THE BROWNINGS
A VICTORIAN IDYLL

ROBERT BROWNING AT 23

" The first poet since Byron who really looks like a poet."

THE
BROWNINGS

A VICTORIAN IDYLL

BY

DAVID LOTH

MCMXXIX

BRENTANO'S·PUBLISHERS

NEW YORK

TO WINK
in all friendship

CONTENTS

CONTENTS

CONTENTS

ILLUSTRATIONS

EUTERPE'S HOLIDAY

EUTERPE *was tired. Never had the Muse of Poetry experienced such complete exhaustion. Lord Byron had reached the depths of degradation and the heights of art, had started a legend that they were on the same level. Euterpe had reached the end of her endurance. Her nerves twitched in most ungoddess-like fashion; her eyes smarted; the skin of her face felt loose and flaccid; her body ached with weariness.*

" No," she cried aloud, " I can't stand it."

Byron looked at her without interest. He had heard so many such cries from so many women. None of them could stand it, he reflected, but one expects more from an immortal. He moved his hands in a feeble gesture of resigned boredom and waited for the deluge.

" Look at us," Euterpe scolded. " You're just as sick of it all as I am. Don't try to pretend with me, not after all these years. Zeus! Thirty years! What other mistress could have held you for thirty years? Not that you haven't at times scorned even me. Oh, I've seen it. A mere Muse isn't good

enough for Your Lordship! You must needs have Aphrodite, and Astarte too. Well, the Gods know you've had your fling at them, and now it brings us here to Venice. You're old at thirty, sick, flabby in body and worse than that in mind. Oh, the bitterness shows in you, you can't escape from the tortures you've inflicted on yourself."

"Myself, myself!" he interrupted hotly. "Did I give myself my genius? Did I make myself and the world I've had to live in? Did I invite the passions and the temptations that have made my life a hell? Why couldn't you let me alone, saved me all these tortures that seem to hurt you so much now? I never knew them to bother you before."

"But don't you see that it's been worth it," the Muse soothed him. "The world can never forget what we have done together. Why, even the blackness that has corroded your heart and soul, all your suffering, your sins and your penances, your pride and your follies are for the world only the dark and lurid frame that sets off as nothing else could the dazzling glory of the picture. For five thousand years I worked to prepare the world for this, and by the Gods I've done it! Once and once only I have translated the true spirit of poetry to the earth that will never see such works as ours again."

For a moment Euterpe's divine grace and beauty returned, for that moment in which she savored again those splendid achievements that stand forever as the Muse's monu-

ment. *Byron himself thrilled to the triumph of her cry, but the moment passed. Her figure slumped and her voice sank. She was a tired goddess who was beginning to show her age.*

" Yes, the grand climax of poesy," she murmured. " But even you can't know what it has cost me. You can't realize what a trying person you are to live with. I'm sick to the death of all this striving to plumb the depths of hell, this desperate dissipation, this eagerness to shock the world by a gaudy display of vice. The moments when we used to rise to God together on the wings of verse are too much for me now. I can't fly any more. I need a rest."

She sighed gustily, but Byron was not deceived. With the wisdom of a man who has witnessed the bursting of many emotional dams, he knew there was more to come. He waited.

" Yes, a rest," Euterpe whispered softly, " a normal, quiet, human life. Zeus, how I long for it! And soon I'll get it, for there is no denying that your time is nearly up. No, don't protest. I have prepared for you such an exit as falls to few men. Life can mean nothing to you any more, and death — well, death means peace for us both. Think, Byron, peace! The peace you might have had in this world but for me and your own passions. The peace you have longed for and never had the strength to grasp. And I too shall find it. Come, I'll show you."

She stretched out a hand and as Byron took it the palace seemed to fall away from them as a cast-off garment; then all Venice, steaming gently in the mist of her canals, vanished, and beneath them the whole world spun slowly past. To the east Missolonghi and Greece darkened and dipped below the wide horizon, but neither Muse nor poet looked that way. Byron was faintly amused to find that, although the earth was spread out like a vast map, yet a steady stare could pick out the most minute details of any neighborhood he fixed upon.

" Your successor, Byron, where shall we look for him? " Euterpe asked as one who humors a sick child.

Below them southern France slid by and Byron pointed to a great chateau.

" No," Euterpe smiled. " I have had enough of the nobility. Look elsewhere."

The poet's brow wrinkled in a scowl. Even an imaginary slight upon the aristocracy to which he was so proud to belong always enraged him, unless of course he gave it himself.

" Well, there then," he snarled. " Perhaps that's the sort of thing you want."

Euterpe glanced down. In a dirty room in the slums of Paris an under-nourished child was regarding gravely the obscene bickerings of his drunken parents. Again Euterpe shook her head.

" I don't feel up to fighting such a battle as he will need to drag him to fame," she explained. " Peace, Byron, peace. That's what I want."

Paris, the coast of France, the Channel, rolled on their way to the sunset and London, big sprawling London, frowned up at them. The poet gasped, then gazed despairingly at the great city to which he could never return. He stared hungrily at drawing-room and club, theater and park, boudoir and coffee-house. Euterpe's eyes searched elsewhere. She smiled wistfully at the comfortable, ugly homes of merchants and clerks, bankers and lawyers, at quiet uneventful places to which poetry was a stranger but where the Muse of Poetry might find a refuge.

She was thinking of this refuge when she saw the boy. With his tongue protruding from one corner of his mouth after the fashion of a little dog that has run too fast, he was writing, slowly but very firmly, some extremely childish verses in labored imitation of Ossian. He finished, drew a deeper breath, sucked his tongue back behind his teeth and tenderly deposited his work under the worn cushions of a big armchair. A considerable cluster of oddly shaped, rather grimy bits of paper was already there, awaiting, the young author hoped, the verdict of posterity.

" Look," Euterpe whispered as her hand clutched Byron's arm. " I've found him."

" Lord, not there," he cried in horror. " Why that's Cam-

berwell, low, middle-class Camberwell! What in the name of all the arts can you expect to find there?"

"Find there! I'll tell you," Euterpe cried furiously. "I'll find happiness." Her tone mocked him. "Only happiness and respectability and a decent self-control. Everything you never had, nothing that will remind me of you in the years to come."

Her voice softened.

"Look, Byron, look at him. Handsome little fellow, isn't he? Not like you, of course, but very nice looking. Clever, too, ambitious in his way, and he will pursue me — I won't always have to be chasing him as I do you. You can't think how divine, how restful it will feel to be worshipped again. How I yearn for it! Sixty or seventy years of a calm, placid, unostentatiously achieving existence. A genuinely happy home to live in, a love — you know, Byron, I shall give that boy a romance so different from any of yours, so different from all others that I know, that the world will remember it long after it has forgotten and ceased to care which of your loves was which.

"He will be happy, healthy, studious, even a scholar. He will have friends as you never did. I shall listen to conversation, not always to wit and satire. A man, not a half-god, half-devil, will follow me — a little way at least — along the paths to glory."

The earth had rolled along quite out of sight, and the

Muse's hand tightened on Byron's again. He closed his eyes as her voice rang in his ears, drowning out the rushing of the wind.

"A man," she repeated, " and peace. By the Gods, it will be a holiday for me, one long happy holiday! I shall end it here in Venice in another palace by the canals, and perhaps I shall remember you then."

When the poet opened his eyes, Euterpe was gone. Only Teresa of the golden hair and opulent figure was with him. He groaned and cursed her, but he never saw the Muse again. She had begun her holiday.

THE BROWNINGS
A VICTORIAN IDYLL

"GENTLEMEN, A TOAST!"

T O the Poets of England!"
Before the speaker could resume his seat cigars were
deposited tenderly on the edge of plates, glasses
clinked and there arose the faint, dull, slightly sheep-
ish mutter which indicates that the festive Britisher is
pleased. Indeed, it was a happy phrase, for the men around
Serjeant Talfourd's well found table were proudly literary,
and most of them could consider the toast a personal
tribute.

The host himself, whose play, "Ion," had that night
been given its *première* in London, was the author of a
dozen ambitious poems, highly praised in their day but
hardly sufficient to prevent their creator from occupying
only the obscure historical niche reserved for the memory
of those who have entertained genius worthily. William
Wordsworth, heir-apparent to the Laureateship, smiled his
placid, faintly ironic smile under his long nose and smoothed
his thick hair back from the bald spot that gave a noble
height to his brow. Walter Savage Landor, bearded, viva-

I

cious, wholly unpredictable, bounced in his chair as he disputed with his neighbors. William Macready, the perfect actor whether on or off the stage, gave a magnificent performance as an English gentleman dining with his friends.

Across from him sat Robert Browning, one of those young men for whom their friends predict great things, and whose writings are casually noticed with conscious condescension by older men. At twenty-three he had already published poems which were rather difficult reading, though none of the men now around him thought any the less of a book because it was hard; they rather welcomed the chance to display their talents for analysis.

Browning was holding up his end of the conversation with eager animation in between the toasts. But at each proposed " health," all men fell silent, for these little interludes were solemn rites, not to be met with levity. There was a growing solemnity about everything in England these days. London that had been so rough and bawdy was settling down to sober respectability, even in its cups. The country was forming new habits to fit the plain, prim young girl who was living in genteel retirement with a strong-willed mother in Kensington House. Not that England paid much attention to the Princess Victoria. An occasional paragraph in the *Gazette* reported her innocent goings and comings for an uninterested public. King William was on the throne — it seemed there never would

be an end to the sons of George the Third — but Victoria and the times were growing up to meet each other.

At Talfourd's house manners took their tone from the more aristocratic society which still rather disdained professional writers. Dinners wound their Epicurean way through the hours to the Port, the goal of any true British meal of the last century. But drinking must have its purpose; the wine, however much it merited the honor, was never its own justification. In order, then, that men might do their tippling with the added relish of knowing they had performed well a moral duty, the drinkers of Old England had invented those vanished phrases: "To the Ladies, God Bless 'Em," "The King," "Confusion to Our Enemies." Gallantry, chivalry and the fine spirit of loyalty to King and country survived in full vigor on a diet of vintage wines.

When a few friends gathered for a little bite, the formalities must be observed. It was the era in which the amenities of life were becoming confused with life itself. Pleasant, too, the guests found it, to feel the warm glow of the wine and the even warmer glow of superiority which their so correct behavior engendered. Talfourd's wines were of the best, and toast had followed toast, with appropriate replies from the guests, while polite murmurs of appreciation for the stilted phrases of the speakers floated upwards with the smoke and dissolved even more quickly into the air.

3

The glasses had been many times refilled when someone remembered that this was a literary gathering and called clearly:

" To the Poets of England! "

Men drank and then glanced expectantly to where Wordsworth and Landor sat on either side of their host, both already choosing among their vast repertoires for the sentences in which they would reply, and both looking just the least bit self-conscious about it. It was a delicate moment for Talfourd, but, though he ate with his knife, he possessed the tact that entertainers of writing men must acquire to meet just such little dilemmas. He bowed to his two most distinguished guests but glanced away from them to call upon " Robert Browning, the youngest of the poets of England." It was a happy touch. Wordsworth smiled benevolently. Browning's lines

" He alone sinks to the rear and the slaves! "

and

" One wrong more to man, one more insult to God! "

had not yet been written. Landor, the violent Latinist whose middle name was rightly " Savage," had for some time been bestowing upon Browning that erratic patronage which led the younger poet to believe that his future as a writer owed more to the lover of Rose Aylmer than to any other man alive. So both the oldsters were well enough pleased as the novice, flushing with pride and pleasure, responded grace-

fully — and what was even more highly approved, briefly — to the toast.

The conversation became general after that, drifted through the arts to the theater where it was captured by Macready, loud in his mournful lamentations concerning the decadence of the modern English drama. The great actor was preparing to embark on his disastrous career as manager, but the disasters were still to come. From his eminence as London's leading man, he surveyed complacently his own vision of the future. In it he could not see a single new play worthy of his talents. Across from him the handsome youth who had responded so well to a toast was speaking quite intelligently of the stage. Macready leaned towards him.

"Write me a play, Browning, and keep me from going to America," he called.

Decidedly it was a great night for the young man. First the chance to respond to a toast — and such a toast — and now this! It was almost too much, but he was never one to spoil his happiness with morbid thoughts on the inescapably sad lot of man, with reflections that we must pay dearly for our triumphs. He seized Macready's gift joyfully and without hesitation.

"Shall it be historical and English?" he asked. "What do you say to a drama on Strafford?"

Macready said yes, and over the wine was thus born Rob-

5

ert Browning, playwright. With the enthusiasm of all the guild, he was almost at once launched upon the career which earned for him a reputation that his admirers are still trying to explain away. Theodore Watts-Dunton, blinded to all other poets by his admiration for Swinburne, was recalling these dramas when, far along in years, he delved into his memories of great Victorians and fished out:

"Oh, yes, Browning. Great diner out. Clever fellow. Too bad he wrote those plays."

THE YOUNG INTELLECTUAL

THE years have a nasty habit of dimming the most glorious triumphs, but even when he was an old man, Browning could savor still the happy moment when the young poet came home to tell his proud family how he had been honored by men of mature years and ripe discrimination. He had a most satisfactory family; they rose splendidly to the occasion, sustaining his own delight in the success that seemed assured.

His father, Bob Browning, the bank clerk, was realizing in his son some of the dreams of his own youth, and he could persuade himself that this sort of vicarious achievement was even better than personal triumphs. Mrs. Browning made up in sincerity what she may have lacked in exuberance as she listened to the story of Macready's invitation. As for the only other child in the family, a younger sister, she had always been an adorer of her clever brother. She was twenty-one, but did not even resent his monopoly of the family good looks.

Play-writing in that household seemed a simple thing.

7

Father and son had only to remember back eighteen years when they were an entire theatrical troupe, extemporizing play, scenery and costumes as they went along. A dependable but not very promising bank clerk and a bright, slightly precocious little boy, they had long ago realized every dream Macready ever had.

Robert never forgot those winter days of 1817 when he had waited so impatiently at the window for Father to come home from the Bank and finish last night's game. No one could play games like Father and no one knew so many games to play. He found a new one between the covers of every book he picked up, and he was always picking up books. They were all over the house, thousands of them, and all so comfortably well worn and thumbed that a few more smudges from a little boy's hands made no difference to anyone.

There were some fresh fingermarks that day in the big book with the funny type that was so hard to read but was necessary to the game, Father said, and Father always knew. At last he was coming, grinning gaily behind his beard. Bob Browning was as enthusiastic about make-believe as any five-year-old in Camberwell. He almost ran the last few steps in his eagerness to get away from the clinging reminders of his day of drudgery in that overpoweringly solemn institution, the Bank of England. Phew! He brushed his hands together and closed the door on reality.

Little Robert (no one abbreviated his name in familiarity
or affection in all his life) ran around in circles whooping.
Mother smiled and went away from the noise of impending
battle. She was not so good at games. Her part in the scheme
of things was to play queer tunes that did something mysterious to her son's insides, to sympathize when he stubbed
a toe, to understand what he could not put into words after
watching the strange world rushing about its business outside the garden.

But now Father was home from the Bank, and the Siege
of Troy could be resumed where it had been interrupted
the night before. Chairs were hastily piled upon tables.

"The topless towers of Ilium," Father explained.

The cat was caught and safely imprisoned behind a ram-
part of books — she played the part of the fair Helen.

"Can't Sis do that?" Robert asked, for he was in a
generous mood.

"We-ell," Father doubted. "You see she's only three. A
little young yet, don't you think?"

So the cat retained her part, and Robert, shouting war
cries, came on with the fierce determination of Achilles
avenging Patroclus. In rapid succession he became Agamem-
non, Ajax, the wily Odysseus and Menelaus. Father kept
pace by rapid metamorphoses into Paris, Hector, Priam.
There were pauses while the contending forces consulted
Mr. Homer's guide-book for the next move; then the clash

9

of arms and shouts of battle resounded again along the plains of Troy and filled the Browning library.

Robert was acquiring scholarship in Greek quite painlessly. His contemporaries wept under the apparent injustice of pedagogues, but Robert only knew that he was having fun. Later he was to learn with astonishment that other boys actually had to be driven to their Greek with blows and threats. Amazing! All his life he was receiving such surprises. He never fully realized the magnitude of the world's ignorance, and the world never forgave him.

But at five years old the only world he knew was that delightful, unsubstantial paradise that lurked within the covers of Father's six thousand books. An eternity of games stretched out before him as he went off reluctantly to bed, bestowing a pitying thought upon the baby sister who had not yet achieved the dignity of a part in the play.

In the library Father put the chairs back on their legs and settled down to a book picked up that very morning, a tattered Italian volume dealing obscurely with the greater obscurities of Guelf and Ghibelline feuds. Father had a passion for such buried bones of information; he could never pass a book-shop without digging for them. Tonight he was not allowed to enjoy the new find.

"Don't you think," Mother asked him, "that we ought to be looking about for a school for Robert?"

"A school!" Father's book dropped on his knees. "No, not for my children. I haven't forgotten my own school-days and what they did to me." His lips puckered for he was tasting bitter memories. "I don't want our son to have a youth like mine. Let him grow up happy."

Bob Browning, whose friends envied him the serenity of his disposition, the quiet excellence of his taste, the unassuming virtuosity of his talents and the happiness of his home, had never been able to get rid of his memories. These barely extended to a dim recollection of his Creole mother, whose shy, sensitive gentleness lived again in the sturdy body of her son.

Margaret Tittle's youth on her father's plantations on St. Kitts had given her only a great timidity and a greater ignorance of everything in the world. The young man who had married her in his quest for a wife who would help him to the fortune that was his goal awed the little colonial. In her humility she could not sufficiently admire the bravado with which he wrested a certain amount of respect and worldly goods from cold, unfriendly London.

This Robert Browning — the family was not original in its choice of names — was a hard-headed man, the son of a yeoman who had come up from Dorsetshire to seek his fortune and had arrived early enough in the rural descent upon the cities to find a clerical post instead of a factory job. The yeoman sent his son to the Bank of England where the young man prospered sufficiently to aspire to the hand of Margaret, West Indian heiress.

Bob Browning, their only child, remembered her vaguely as a quiet person who told him stories of a girlhood on the sugar plantations. During his school-days the faint vision of a West Indian panorama, the blacks singing at their work in the cane, the white masters living in luxurious isolation, the unreal beauty of tropical islands, seemed to be something he had once seen himself.

Margaret died young, leaving a harsh disciplinarian of a husband to crush if he could the mild but tenacious sympathy for others which was their child's chief characteristic.

The father, his serious attentions divided between his pleasant duties as a superior Bank of England official and the courting of a second wife, packed the boy off to one of those public schools which were learning the knack of molding even the most unlikely human material nearer to the cold, imperial indifference which was the national heart's desire.

The man who emerged from this probably excellent institution of its brutal kind always exaggerated the boy's sufferings. Memories of friendships and triumphs could not dim the horror with which he regarded his own youth. He had enjoyed sports and been good at them; he had relished the petty successes of leadership in and out of classrooms, but he could never lose his gentleness, his fastidious, in-

stinctive affection for everything and everyone he saw. Even
the careless brutality of the English schoolboy only saddened,
could not embitter him.

He left Cheshunt School with more than a youth's normal
joy in emancipation, but he returned to a home dominated
by a young stepmother whose only care was to keep her
stern, devoted, elderly husband's affections centered on her
own brood of small children. The Creole's son, it was made
abundantly plain to him, was an intruder.

At nineteen he was a distinct problem in a household
given over to consolidating the family position in life. The
youth was romantic, but that might have been tolerated
had he not added the reprehensible ambition of becoming
a painter. He possessed a talent for drawing which his
father considered effeminate.

Browning senior scoffed cruelly and dispatched his son
to the West Indies to learn something useful, the manage-
ment of the rich estate his mother had left him. The disap-
pointments of Bob's English career dissolved into the morning mist as his ship approached St. Kitts — drowsing; exotic;
gorgeously, tenderly, hotly seductive; worthy of any man's
passionate adoration. He rode over his plantations enfolded
in a warm delight of dreams, imagining a paradise that he
would build. He planned happily until one day he realized
that his paradise upreared its gaudy splendors from the hell
of slavery. After that St. Kitts was spoiled for him.

Men like Bob Browning, full of fanatical zeal for abstract justice, were peculiarly susceptible just then to the glorious, ennobling, resounding but empty shibboleths that poured out of revolutionary France on waves of insane enthusiasm and with the compelling force that Holy Writ had lost.

Many were content to be lulled by the hollow calls of liberty and fraternity. Browning insisted upon a practical demonstration of his belief, so typical of his day, that man is born to freedom. Freedom was not yet so common that anyone thought to ask what should be done with it. This one young idealist, nauseated by the source of his wealth, freed every slave he owned and parcelled out among them the fruitful plantations of his maternal heritage. His fellow landowners cursed his betrayal of class interests, but their fury was easily avoided. He sailed for home, leaving the planters of St. Kitts to draw closer together against the dangerous liberalism of new ideas.

The anger he left behind him was nothing to the rage that greeted him at home. His old Tory of a father, now retired from the Bank, solacing himself with domesticity and righteous, imperialistic outbursts against the fiend Napoleon, welcomed the prodigal with a venom that combined the planter's hatred of a traitor with the banker's hatred of a wastrel.

He issued a plain warning that the son should henceforth

keep out of the Browning house. That paternal gesture, however, was not enough to satisfy his outraged feelings, and he sent to the boy's new lodgings a statement of accounts due. The old financier started it off with the hospital bill incurred during his first wife's confinement. Board and lodgings for twenty years, books, clothing, tuition, tips and presents were carefully itemized. It was typical of the pride of youth and the implacability of age that Bob Browning used the last shilling of his mother's fortune to pay the bill and his father pocketed the money without adding the usual thanks to his formal receipt.

The younger man's vein of kindness was proof against even these shocks. Paint and canvas still lured him, and he had planned to use for the study of art the money his father had taken. There was no chance of more schooling now. According to all tradition, Bob Browning should have dragged a bitter soul through starvation, frustration and misery in a garret, sneering at the success of other men and nursing his own failure as the reward of great genius.

Instead he fell in love. Sarah Ann was the daughter of William Wiedemann, of Hamburg, a shipowner who had married a Scotch girl and settled in Dundee. For her Bob relinquished his dreams and went to work. They were to be married as soon as he had an income which by the unexacting standards of the time was adequate for a

young couple. Old Browning heard of it and was displeased on principle.

"My son is obviously born to be hanged. I would warn you not to let your daughter have anything to do with him," he advised Wiedemann, assuming the expression of a man who gives disinterested advice, but unable to keep his voice on the same calm level.

Wiedemann listened politely, but he much preferred the son to the father. The youngsters were married not long afterwards, for Bob had obtained a place in the Bank of England, the only source of jobs he knew. He got it quite easily, for he was his father's son, and the old man's opinion of him had not penetrated to the Bank. For a young Browning, the officials said, there was always a clerkship, and upon that work Bob lavished a lifetime of conscientious, dutiful attention. Save for his books and his facility in caricature he could hardly have been distinguished from any one of a thousand other bank clerks passing his days peacefully between his office and his home.

His children would have more than compensated him for the sacrifice of the artist's life he had meant to lead, even if he had ever been conscious of having made a sacrifice. Any children would have done that, for he was one of those maternal men whose ineradicable innocence finds its only truly congenial companions in the innocence of childhood. But little Robert and Sarianna were unusually delightful chil-

dren, their father thought. One of his greatest pleasures consisted in retailing to politely inattentive acquaintances the latest feats of his offspring.

But he much preferred the hours spent in fighting over again with Robert the heroic battles of antiquity. For quieter seasons he dragged out from the musty corners of his vast scholarship tales of forgotten Persian princelings, unknown Renaissance artists, Arab philosophers, Italian politicians, Hebrew students. While his Camberwell playmates were begging for bedtime stories, Robert absorbed, just as voraciously, more history than would have been good for an Oxford Don. Bob Browning's idea of proper fairy tales for the growing boy was responsible for turning loose upon the world a poet who never knew that these were not the fairy tales of all men's childhood. What, not know that "Mansoor" was one of the names of the third Vatemite Caliph, Biamvallah? Such ignorance amounted to illiteracy. Every child, at least every Browning child, knew that.

In the comfortable old house in Camberwell, then a region of homes and gardens, now degenerated into the hideous congestion of a great city's carelessness, Robert Browning was acquiring at five years of age that strong, unconscious love of learning and those satisfying domestic virtues that never left him. Childhood's right to happiness was granted him so lavishly that sixty years later there was another word besides " Italy " graven upon his heart. Famous at last, the story of his Italian idyll known to all of the world that he cared about, avid for recognition by that British public which had so long ignored him, he was back in England, luxuriating expansively in the adulation he had waited a generation to obtain and hearing from the lips of a smug young admirer:

" There is no romance now except in Italy."

The poet smiled, but not in agreement. He was thinking of those golden days when he and Sis and Father were all children together in the happy land of dreams closed forever to literary critics, jealous authors and members of Browning Societies.

" Ah, well," he replied wistfully, " I should like to include poor old Camberwell."

The romance of Camberwell was more in the poet's mind than in his experience, in spite of the entry in his childish diary: " Married two wives this morning." The peace of a soul-satisfying, uneventful happiness was what the poet confused with romance, unless he remembered Abel, the music master, as a romantic figure. For Abel was a sentimentalist and interrupted the music lessons in the old house to unfold to an interested but uncomprehending boy the turbulent passions of his current love affair. For more than twenty years the word " love " evoked in Robert's brain the image of the young teacher analyzing his own emotions.

" Yes," Abel would confide to the sympathetic pupil, " it

destroys my appetite, interferes with my sleep and considerably breaks in upon my practising."

From this love-sick soul Robert derived the foundation on which he built a prodigious scholarship of music, pleasantly leavened with sufficient virtuosity to enable him to amuse a drawing-room. It was characteristic of him to brag about qualities for which he was not remarkable. Although singularly and sincerely modest about his writing, save for quite rare confidences to a few intimates, he bragged not a little of his health, his strength, his manners (which were really nothing to boast about), his modelling, his sketching and his music.

" I was," he once asserted to clinch an argument, " studying the grammar of music when most children were learning the multiplication table, and I know what I am talking about when I speak of music."

His mother was responsible for his musical inclinations. The one inviolable family rule was that which insured Mrs. Browning an hour of absolute solitude at dusk. In that hour, seated at the piano, she gave the only expression that ever escaped her to the mysticism of her Scotch-German nature. Her son's earliest recollections were of listening to her playing and of crying for more. For the rest she was a very silent person, commanding in that household of unending conversation the exaggerated respect which garrulous mortals always bestow upon those with a gift for holding their

tongues. Robert repaid her willingness to listen with a profound devotion. Her quiet calm seemed to him much more admirable than his father's demonstrative affection, unfailing generosity and genius at playing games.

In spite of Bob's prejudices, the time came for Robert to learn the multiplication table as well as music. He was ten years old when he started as a day boy at the Reverend Thomas Read's school in the neighborhood. In his four years at this institution of learning he was neither a conspicuous success nor a horrible example. He occupied the unobtrusive middle ground which is so pleasing to teachers who must base their efforts on the intangible qualities of " the average student." When he was fourteen Robert left the school without regrets on either side. His formal education, save for some stray Greek lectures at the University of London, was complete.

Meanwhile Father's friends were beginning to take an interest in the boy, and these friends were men from whom such notice was the equivalent of laurel and bay and a guarantee of royal pension. John Stuart Mill deigned to glance over some verses forced upon him by a proud parent, and the old economist's praises, valued in literary circles, were more lavish than mere politeness dictated. But he added the comment:

" The writer possesses a deeper self-consciousness than I ever knew in a sane human being."

Of course the boy was very much a cub. He became a vegetarian. He discovered Shelley all by himself, and in honor of the treasured volume entitled " Mr. Shelley's Atheistical Poems " picked up in a second-hand bookstore, he turned against the God of his chapel-going ancestors. Shelley was in eclipse just then. His life was remembered by those who prided themselves on keeping up with the scandals of the upper classes, but his poetry was ignored. Robert's own pride as a discoverer gave him a lasting admiration for the poet and a temporary faith in vegetarianism and atheism.

He recovered from both these ailments of youth quickly, especially from the first which made him slightly ill. Then, as the first faint smudge of whisker beclouded his swarthy good looks and his body lost its gangling awkwardness in a slender grace which he cultivated assiduously, he devoted himself seriously to the arts of boxing, riding, fencing and dancing. He speculated, with less absorption, on the choice of a career. The indulgence of an adoring father opened to him all lines of human endeavor. The law, diplomacy and literature presented attractions to the boy, but there was no hurry. Life was very sweet in Camberwell. Why work when, without it, all that a man desires is gladly granted?

So Robert pursued his books and his sports. He developed a loud voice and a bumptious manner. He displayed with a most unpleasant assurance his unusual learning and with equal arrogance his more ordinary talents. In a lordly way he and a few other young sprigs settled with ease and to their own satisfaction those questions of politics and philosophy, the propounding of which were ushering in the glories of the Victorian Age. Daily the young Moses descended upon his family from Sinai with new tablets of stone until even his patient mother remonstrated and the hitherto admiring Sis fled at his approach. In a word, he was eighteen.

Time cured him of that as it had cured him of vegetarianism and atheism, and he recovered with the same facility from his admiration for law, a cure that carried with it complete immunity from another attack. There remained only a choice of those leisurely callings, diplomacy and literature. But still there was no hurry. No matter which he chose, it was certain Father would be called upon to support him for a good few years to come.

THREE

A MAN OF FASHION

ROBERT was reading Dr. Johnson's dictionary through from beginning to end, but despite this mastery of a necessary prerequisite, there was little conscious choice in his drift to literature.

He was one of those unfortunates who are incapable of enjoying complete idleness, and his nervous energy found an outlet in poetry more easily than in any other intellectual enterprise. He wrote verses as naturally as he talked; the gift of rhyming that was born in him had developed out of all proportion, and as the joys and sorrows, hopes and fears, belief and disbelieving of youth tumbled in wild confusion through his brain he tried to capture his vague aspirations on paper.

He called the attempt "Pauline" and through the remainder of a long life enjoyed a healthy contempt for this work of his immaturity. It had length, indeed, and a certain something which hinted to men of rare discernment that its author was more gifted than a superficial reading would indicate. An indulgent aunt, Mrs. Silverthorne, whose son

was one of Robert's intimates in those ardent discussions about the significance of Life and Art, paid for the publication of " Pauline." It appeared just after Robert's twenty-first birthday in an anonymity for which he remained eternally grateful. The book, however, had enough of his characteristic style that Rossetti, happening on it in the British Museum years later, remarked that only Browning could have written it.

Rossetti liked it, and at the time of publication Bob's journalistic friend, Mr. Fox, gave the young poet a strong boost in his *Monthly Repository*. The one or two other reviews that noticed " Pauline " at all were indifferent. They did not even accord it the serious denunciation which Robert was later to look upon as the sincerest form of flattery. Most of the literary magazines completely ignored the new writer, and their example was followed by the reading public. Not a single copy of " Pauline's " first edition found a buyer.

But in 1833 an author's claim to recognition was not based on his publisher's account sheet. Though no book of its generation fell quite so flat from the financial point of view as " Pauline," its appearance was enough to make Robert definitely and forever a poet. Father stood by loyally with encouragement, advice, influence — and money. He was proud to be supporting a poet.

As a man committed to literature, Robert was welcomed to the fringe of literary society. It was his element. The talk

of books and philosophies about which he knew and could talk back, the fascinating study of men and women, the first exhilarating contacts with people outside the immediate circle of his home and early friends — these pleasures crowded thick upon the young lover of life. He absorbed them all greedily, seeking in the murkiness of London to gratify his tastes for the unusual, for strong but not profane language, good, rich, mouth-filling words, for spectacles all a blaze of gaudy color, for stories of body and blood.

However, he had always known there was a wider and more satisfactory world than London, and this same year he began to travel. George de Benkhausen, the Russian Consul General, wanted a companion for his long journey home badly enough to say he needed a secretary (unpaid). Robert got the job and departed in an ecstasy of anticipation which for once was unspoiled by the realization.

Everything entranced him, the long drive fifteen hundred miles across Europe, the halts at obscure villages to change horses, the helpful interest of the peasantry, the strange scenery and at last Russia, her vast level expanses made vivid by semi-oriental customs, made monotonous by snows and long silences as they crawled at what Robert thought a recklessly rapid pace over the white countryside.

When the Czar drank the first water from the Neva after the ice broke, the picturesque ceremony, rich in the fascination of a tradition centuries old, threw Robert into raptures.

So did the wildly tragic stories of Russian heroes told interminably around the leaping night fires. So did the steaming fish pies sold in the market places. If all foreign countries offered such entertainment, he reflected, there might yet be reason to embrace a diplomatic career. Diplomats see the world. He returned home, overflowing with the enthusiasm of the traveller with an audience, and applied for a post in Persia. It was denied him, so again he abandoned himself to poetry and Society.

Mr. Fox accepted a few short pieces for his *Repository* and Robert had his first readers. He was also flying a little higher in Society and in these rarefied heights he encountered Count Amédée de Ripert-Monclar, a Bourbon sympathizer and a dilettante of literature who despised poor old Louis Philippe as much for his unimaginativeness as for his revolution. From the Count Robert received the suggestion for a poem on Paracelsus, that poor mediaeval struggler after the truth who was diversely appreciated — by the few who had ever heard of him— as the father of all science and the father of all quacks.

Here was the sort of subject no Browning could resist. Father had a mine of information hidden away in forgotten corners of his mind. His son, never Bob's equal in learning but always his superior in method, hurried to the British Museum. Browsing happily in the dust of antiquity, he decided that the actual facts of Paracelsus's strange career were

well enough known — an illusion so ridiculous as to merit
the suspicion of insanity in any man less oddly educated. But
Robert, if he thought about it at all, actually believed the
whole world knew everything that was a secret between
himself and the British Museum. He felt that there remained
for him only to record the pilgrimage over a troubled earth
of Paracelsus's troubled soul, a theme which appealed to
him much more strongly than any mere record of a man's
actions.

Monclar, who shared the early labors of research, was appalled by the mass of dry, pseudo-scientific information they
had stirred up. In it all there was not a single shred of love
interest! The Count, his clear French glance perceiving at
once the impossibility of a successful poem devoid of tender
passion, tried to drag his young friend from his musty
studies. He failed, for Robert Browning, turning over the
fragile leaves of old books by day and pacing the woods
around Dulwich by night, was attaining his stature as a full-
grown poet. All day long he shovelled into his brain the
dead stalks of mediaeval scholarship. At night as he walked
under the trees, the stalks came alive in a ferment of im-
agery and he chanted softly to himself in the verse he would
put down on paper as soon as he got home. Love interest!
Bah! He would show the world how completely unneces-
sary love interest is to the creation of poetry.

"Paracelsus" was published with Father's money and

dedicated to Monclar. Both the author and his friend were proved right. As a book to be bought and read, " Paracelsus " fared little better than " Pauline." As proof of poetic power it was a triumphant vindication of Bob Browning's good nature and tolerance, for it placed his son forever among the writers whom writers read.

It did more. It won for the young poet — he was not quite twenty-four — the friendship of men who were building a new Golden Age of English letters. It opened for him the doors of that more glittering Society which aspired to a patronage of the arts. Even the august portals of Lady Blessington's might not close in front of the bank clerk's son. He was invited to all sorts of houses, for Society was curious indeed to see what the new poet-philosopher, whom they had not read, looked like.

" Why! " exclaimed Society in glad amazement, " he's handsome! The first poet since Byron who really looks like a poet! "

He was so young, so charmingly, poignantly young, to have written a book from whose learning a superficial public shrank. Big gray eyes under a high, wide brow looked innocently and brightly upon a world which had a sneaking affection for innocence — Victorian days were not yet. Well-shaped, sensitive lips curved in a smile of happiness upon all men, and all men, even the sourest, were constrained to smile back. A mop of glossy, nearly black hair fell from the brow

in waves of Byronic splendor, and the smooth features were surrounded stylishly by a framework of curly whisker after the fashion which Greeley was to make famous across the Atlantic.

Young Browning's excellent figure rivalled that of the dandy, Disraeli, even in the modishness of its garb. Young Mr. Browning's waistcoats were not so splendidly flowered, but his gloves were an even more brilliant shade of yellow. A girl who saw him performing at the piano one day recorded the startling fact that he was " quite the glass of fashion and the mould of form." A little loud, Society thought, perhaps a trifle on the vain side, but undeniably good-looking, and how the boy could dance! Invitations were repeated.

For Robert the London of 1835 was a Garden of Eden where the critic serpents had not yet raised their heads. They had stirred a little restlessly under the barrage of Paracelsus's phrases, but they had not struck venomously. They were not accustomed to thoughtful poetry. They rebelled against admitting that a man might be able to think and at the same time express his thoughts in verse. They laughed a little at the upstart and turned to praise a new French grammar that was really of some value.

Any one of them would have been amazed to learn that the book they praised and the book they scorned were the work of the same man. Robert's old French teacher had provided the substance of the grammar and the pupil, always

ready to place his talents at the disposal of a friend, had written the book without thinking it at all strange that two such opposite works should come from the same pen at the same time.

In lay circles the only adulation the author of " Paracelsus " received for his ability was from the venerable *Lancet,* which put him on a high pedestal just to be able to knock him down with a more destructive crash.

" Here in England," wrote the medical critic in an article denouncing quacks, " we have Browning, a prince of poets, touching the pitch which defiles and making Paracelsus the hero of a poem."

Despite such comments the circle of dear, early friends was widening to include more imposing figures. Old Mr. Fox was very kind about "Paracelsus" in the *Repository.* John Forster started a beautiful friendship with a piece in the revered *Examiner.* Carlyle found enough philosophy in the book to urge the author to abandon poetry for an intelligible form of expression. Wordsworth was condescending; Landor unbent; Monckton-Milnes admired; Leigh Hunt dissertated in lively counsel, and William Macready, translating his emotions into the thoughts of his beloved theatre, exclaimed:

" He looks and speaks more like a young poet than anyone I have ever seen."

With such men as familiars, seen daily at hospitable tables,

listened to by them, talked to, walked with — living always on Parnassus, what mattered it if the poor dear British public did obstinately refuse to read Browning? He was enjoying a sweeter triumph than any pack of fools yelping admiringly at his heels could provide. He was a part of London.

And such a London! The old city was bursting the bonds of more feudal days as the great middle class, astonished and excited by its own achievements, rose towards the pinnacle of magnificence it was to achieve under the long rule of the ignored Princess Victoria. Reform, after the battles of political giants, seemed to be settled forever; the Tories had become Conservatives and newer, greater political giants were winning their spurs for the imperial crusade they would undertake on behalf of mediocrity.

Lord Melbourne, very wise, very mild, gently witty and always a little sad, crowned the political heap. Lady Blessington and Lady Howard disputed delightfully for the social honor of bankrupting themselves to provide the wits and scholars of the town with a field on which to display their talents. Lady Blessington won. A young man named Charles Dickens, well known to the newspaper editors of the day, was acquiring complete mastery of a new art. In less than a year London would be fighting in the streets for the next installment of Mr. Pickwick's adventures and forgetting the niceties of Lord Palmerston's foreign policy in excited argu-

ment about the likelihood of the more lovable gentleman's escape from a debtor's prison.

In the homes of the mighty, gentlemen over their wine discoursed of the splendid liberal movement of which they were all proud to be a part. Universal happiness was such a simple matter in 1835. The untrammelled right of the masses to vote for the ruling class — the phrase had meaning then, for where else could you find culture, brains, poise and statesmanship? — and complete liberty to starve in the shameful slums of a new industrialism seemed to be the passports to a bourgeois paradise which was just around the corner. Emancipation, freedom, expansion — these were the words men used as, mercifully denied the spirit of prophecy, they babbled on in glowing terms concerning England's future and mankind's redemption.

In this world of politeness and conversation literary reputations were won and lost. For a young man who could talk charmingly, with just enough wit to be entertaining and not so much as to be nasty, who could make music and sketch an amusing caricature — a gift acquired from his father — and could hold his own on the dance floor with any man in London, this was the world in which to shine. It was much better than to depend for recognition on the few who read his books. The respect of the charming people he met at dinner parties was more valuable than the praise of his literary peers.

In all this world of men and women, however, young Browning found no inspiration for his muse. Instead he was projecting a poem about an obscure Italian poet when he could spare the time from dinners and balls and calls, the long walks and rides, the theaters and coffee-houses. They were months filled with dreams as old King William, unhonored and unmourned, withdrew from the world and made way for the little girl in Kensington House. The great Victorian Age had dawned at last. The great middle class of England had found its idol.

Before that happened, the lure of the theater possessed Robert with all the force which the stage's glamor can exert upon a youth of twenty-four. Macready was his friend; he knew Charles Kean and the Kembles. He had seen players skillfully twisting the hearts of sobbing audiences, drawing them back to laughter, exalting them above the world. Here, ready to his hand, was the tool for ennobling a public that refused to buy books but might come to the theater. All the high talk of the dinner tables could be redistilled, refined and poured out upon enthralled spectators in a torrent of poetry. After all, poetry was made to be heard, not read.

He was learning the power of the spoken word in other ways, too. He was listened to with respect now, for he no longer tried to dominate the talk. The young poet was acquiring the charm, tolerance and ease of manner that were to make him one of the most delightful dinner guests in London, recognized as such even by those who were inexpressibly bored by his books.

So stage fever had burned in Robert's brain long before the night at Talfourd's when he sat across from Wordsworth and Landor and Macready, responding to toasts and elaborating a theory that men reached the highest exaltation to which art could transport them when they listened to noble blank verse describing magnificent deeds and eloquently spoken by actors of good presence and rolling voices.

FOUR

THE PLAYWRIGHT

THE project of a play was not new. In the intervals of work on his new Italian poem, Robert had been thinking of a drama about Narses, the eunuch general whose distorted affections, centering on gold and a pious adoration of the Virgin, presented the sort of psychological theme Robert most desired. To give a more obviously dramatic effect there was also to be woven into the plot the story of how Narses saved Justinian's throne only to revenge the succeeding Emperor's jibe, " Send him back to the women where such as he belong," by loosing the Lombard barbarians upon an Italy he had ruled for years.

But more recent labors put Narses out of Robert's mind in favor of Strafford. John Forster was writing a life of the Earl of Wentworth who lost his head trying to save Charles the First from the consequences of the monarch's own duplicity. Forster had enlisted Robert's historical talents and the Browning family's store of obscure facts in the interests of his book. For weeks Robert had been living at the Stuart court, seeing it all with the eyes of Strafford, more and more

fascinated by the romance of a strong man's fight for a weak master.

Macready liked the idea, so Robert pushed aside the scribbled sheets of his Italian poem and began turning out the play. It promised so well that Macready boasted to his diary that he had "awakened a spirit of poetry whose influence would elevate, ennoble and adorn our degraded drama." Robert spent a great deal of his time at the actor's home, full of confidence in himself, his play, his friends and his future. The actor's praises spurred him on.

The Brownings had moved from Camberwell to Hatcham, and in the comfortable, low-ceilinged rooms of New Cross, surrounded by Father's books, Robert rejoiced in composition. Beside him Sis, trained as the perfect amanuensis, copied in a fair hand the crabbed scrawl which her brother himself could hardly read. In the stable Uncle Reuben's horse waited to be exercised. Reuben was almost part of the family, as the Brownings had been reconciled a few years before the old financier died. He relented at last when he saw that Bob's life had been proof that he would never revert to the prodigal ambitions of his youth.

Looking out over the Surrey hills, Robert revelled in the "depressing optimism" which Tennyson called his greatest fault. Even as a young man he had developed strongly the impudent disregard of mortality which insured the serenity of his long life and enabled him to say with sincere asperity:

" Never say of me that I am dead."

He produced his drama slowly despite the ardor with which he entered on the work. There were many distractions. Dinners and rides, visitors who came to see the author of " Paracelsus " and remained to be " tea-ed " by Mrs. Browning and entertained by the poet's father, long idle days with Arnould and Dommett and Silverthorne, the friends of his childhood — all these kept him often from his desk. Sis had plenty of time to herself.

Strafford was not finished until nearly a year after Talfourd's dinner. Macready immediately began rehearsals, that process by which a playwright's heart is broken and he is subjected to the producer's will. Macready's enthusiasm for the manuscript changed to perverse and harshly worded criticism. The play did not seem to act as well as it read, and the actor-manager had no scruples about changing it. Robert for the first time was seeing his genial host and kind friend engaged in real work. The Macready of the dinner table bore no resemblance to this savage who stormed over the bare stage tearing at " Strafford's " vitals to create an entertainment. Robert watched and wondered, and even protested vainly, but the manager of the theater, a shrewd little man named Osbaldiston, reassured the puzzled author. He promised Robert twelve pounds a night for the first twenty-five nights and ten pounds for each of the succeeding ten performances if the play should have so long a run. It was big money, but Macready was determined to put the theater on a sound footing with legitimate, first-rate shows. No expense was to be spared.

For when, in his bitterness, Macready referred to " our degraded drama " he did not exaggerate. The London stage of the thirties, adorned though it was by Macready, the Keans, the Kembles, Helen Faucit and a dozen others, was disgraced every time it strayed away from Shakespeare. Covent Garden and Drury Lane, the national theaters, struggled against an indifferent public to maintain the traditions of the classic drama. Haymarket, the only other stage of consequence, was sunk to circus parades and the cheapest mummery of the music halls. Bad imitations of the Greek were the best the playwrights of the day could produce, and even the Greeks themselves were no longer attracting audiences.

Producers, as producers will, caught at the popular taste. Alfred Bunn, who had been Macready's manager until a quarrel sent the actor out on his own, saved a dismal tragedy called " Charlemagne " by introducing into its dolorously dignified scenes what his hand-bills described as " a double stud of highly trained palfreys and Mr. Van Amburgh's celebrated lions." The young Victoria came six times in six weeks to see the lions, applauding prettily from the royal box, and an adoring public took its cue from the palace. Bunn packed 'em into Drury Lane to the sweetly sounding

tune of seven hundred pounds a night while poor Macready
was lucky to find two hundred in the box office at Covent
Garden when it came time to count up.

His disappointment added to his asperity as " Strafford "
struggled on towards the first night. More and more be-
wildered by the labors attending the birth of his first play,
Robert discovered within himself the seeds of a temper
which nothing in all his twenty-five years had ever roused.
He was so disgusted with the confusion of the dress re-
hearsal that on the night of May first when " Strafford "
opened he was at home, salving his dismay with plans for
future writings. He had never heard of the proverbial difference between dress rehearsals and first nights.

The little triumph when it came was, therefore, all the
more uplifting. He did not see Macready's magnificent work
in the title rôle; he missed Helen Faucit's charm as Lady
Carlisle. He was able to take as a personal tribute the more
than kindly criticisms, which after all had been written by
his and Macready's friends. Robert wrote the critics long,
grateful letters and saw the second performance before a
packed house. After all the torments of disillusion, his
dreams had come true.

But not Macready's. The show's appeal seemed to be dis-
tinctly limited. The houses dwindled; the man who played
Pym deserted the cast, and " Strafford's " fifth night was its
last. The play that had been written to save Macready from

39

going to America died on the very day that the actor-manager accepted an offer from New York.

Its moment of favor was, however, enough to secure its publication, the first of Robert's works to appear at the publisher's risk. Longman regretted taking the risk when he saw the sales report, but Robert consoled himself with the thought that in two and a half years Tennyson's last volume had sold only three hundred copies.

Meanwhile Robert returned to the discarded Italian poem. All through the winter he piled obscurity upon obscurity, burrowing deeper and deeper into another poet's soul and closing the tunnel behind him. The style was growing on him. He wrote long letters to his publishers which they could not understand; his most casual correspondence became a maze of intricate phraseology that frequently defied analysis and which his unique ideas on punctuation did nothing to untangle. But he could still talk plainly enough, and the Italian poem suffered delay, as " Strafford " had done, from his incurable sociability.

He was frequently to be found at the Carlyles. His admiration for the philosopher of Cheyne Row was boundless. Standing on the hearth rug he declaimed for hours at the wasted, sorrowful countenance of his host or listened respectfully to an answering shower of rolling R's as Carlyle poured forth his wisdom. On other days Carlyle rode out to New Cross and discovered in his young friend's mother

ROBERT BROWNING

The Greatest Diner-Out in London.

the finest type of Scottish womanhood. She did not talk much, she made her guests comfortable, and the unhappy author found in the felicity of the Browning home a peace that could never exist in a household of which he was the master.

Nor, for that matter, of which his Jane was the mistress. Robert was always a passionate defender of the husband in the gossip which it was inevitable the Carlyles should provoke. So much genius, he contended, was entitled to wifely indulgence. Robert did not know how trying genius could be. Besides, he had never read Jane Welsh's letters and could not know that she had the same quality. He remembered her best as (oh, damning, damning phrase!) the unladylike virago who had made such stinging remarks the day he burned a hole in her new rug with a hot teakettle. She had quite spoiled one of his best stories, and never had much use for him thereafter. Anyway, Robert's devotion to his friends prevented his taking a detached attitude; he would have regarded as disloyalty any acquiescence in criticism of the husband. He could not share the calm cynicism of Tennyson, who commented on someone's regret that Thomas Carlyle and Jane Welsh had ever married:

" Not at all. This way there are only two unhappy people instead of four."

Even more than Cheyne Row, the gayer society of fashionable routs claimed evenings that might have been devoted

to writing. Robert could not stay away from balls, even though he might return in the sunshine of next day complaining bitterly about women who danced badly. He was particular about his partners and once commented with feeling on his misfortune in getting within the space of a single evening " one lady whose head could not, and another whose feet could not, dance." London was very gay that winter, Victoria's first on the throne, and there was no lack of opportunity for the young poet to display his graces upon the dance floor.

Spring found the poem still uncompleted. But the delay was fortunate. Father thought his son might well travel in Italy and, as Robert put it, in a fond belief that what he was writing was intelligible, " finish my poem amidst the scenes it describes." Carefully provided with the proper trappings of a young English gentleman bound for the Continent, he was seen safely aboard ship for Trieste.

It was a glorious voyage at the start, and Robert, the only passenger aboard, acquired a nautical vocabulary which pervaded his letters for months. But storms met the good ship Norham Castle off the Bay of Biscay and Robert was very sick. Kind Captain Davidson supported him to the deck to see Gibraltar towering ahead, but Robert failed just then to appreciate the rough majesty of the rock. He was exploring the depths of *mal de mer* which produced a few days later the feeling lines, " Home Thoughts from the Sea."

The Mediterranean was gentler than the Atlantic. It provided calm seas and even an adventure, for off Algiers the Norham Castle picked up an overturned French smuggler. When righted, the damaged hulk gave up a half dozen month-old corpses, a surprising quantity of tobacco and cloth and a stench that caused Captain Davidson to fear his men, who promptly began to loot the cigars, might bring the plague aboard his ship. So in the night the Norham Castle sailed away from the unclean derelict, but not before Robert had seized as souvenirs two cutlasses, a dagger and the memory of one putrefying pirate lying on the filthy deck, " his hands clasped as if praying."

A few weeks later the young tourist was confessing that he had fallen in love with Italy. It was the Italy of the Hapsburgs, all the dearer because oppressed. The old appeal of beauty in distress captured the sentiment of Englishmen. Furthermore it was Spring in Asolo and Robert was twenty-six. The graver was at work on his heart, and in the fullness of his love he waxed almost coherent, a quality that even the love of woman could not bestow upon his letters.

It was the only visit he ever made as a typical English tourist. He met few Italians, though he liked those few. Most of his time went to admiration of the scenery as he passed from town to town and of the glories of Italian art. Bob Browning had done his work well; his son knew a good

picture when he saw it, and for the first time since he had haunted the Dulwich Gallery as a child he was able to indulge his fondness for paintings. Everywhere he went he was intoxicated with the splendid recklessness with which nature and Italian artists splashed their colors. He could not get enough of it, for he loved his colors bright and thick, but at last, reluctantly, he rode north through the mountains, marvelling to see such splendors, through Germany and Belgium and so back to England.

He brought with him a new parlor trick. Select audiences were entertained by seeing the author of " Paracelsus " smoke a bit of paper over the candles and then etch on the mottled surface with a dry pen scenes from the hills above Asolo, palaces on the Grand Canal, types of peasant faces. It was very diverting and Robert became an even more popular dinner guest than before.

At Talfourd's one night — how that good man's table seemed to be a focus for all the molding influences of Robert's life — he fell into conversation with a sprightly, gray-headed man who studied the effect of his own wit with a keenly inquiring twinkle of spectacles. As they were introduced, the older man commented upon what he regarded as the coincidence of Robert's name. Could it be that his father's name was Robert, too? Had his father attended Mr. Bell's school at Cheshunt? Well, Robert should ask if Bob remembered John Kenyon from Cheshunt. Remember him?

Bob could draw his face so accurately that Robert recognized the boy's likeness to the man.

Kenyon came to New Cross to renew the memories of his youth, and Robert learned the origin of those games that had made the library in Camberwell a boy's paradise. Bob had relieved the nightmare of his school-days by organizing sham battles on a huge scale, and Kenyon had always been his chief lieutenant. The old friend, now pursuing the serious and arduous occupation of man about town, liked Robert. Almost from their first meeting he began the series of generosities which were to earn for him Robert's cry of enthusiastic gratitude:

" He deserves to be known as Kenyon the Magnificent."

That idea would have astonished fashionable London where for years the object of Robert's superlatives had been giving and attending the most severely correct type of literary dinners, writing politely ardent verses to Lady Blessington and publishing poems which the reviewers, all grateful for favors received, were able without shame to describe as " good manly works." On his reputation as litterateur, wit and patron of arts, Kenyon buzzed happily about the town, singing the praises of his friends. He had an enviable capacity for real appreciation. Wordsworth made the Kenyon house his London home. Southey and Landor were familiars. The works of Browning and Tennyson were accorded equal places of honor. A host of forgotten versifiers repaid with a profound ingratitude the substantial encouragement of " the Magnificent."

Robert, too, was a lover of other men's poetry. He admired, but never envied, the simplicity of Wordsworth, and lived to regret his action " in my hasty youth " in selecting the Laureate for the title rôle of " The Lost Leader." He gave unreserved praise to Tennyson, who returned the compliment, and their intercourse was carried out on a high plane of mutual regard, much as if the North and South Poles could be heard congratulating each other on their difficulty of access.

Kenyon had an invalid cousin whose poetic star was rising, and he was gratified to find in Robert a proper respect for the works of Miss Elizabeth Barrett.

Meanwhile the Italian poem was completed and in the early Spring of 1840 " Sordello " was launched upon a world that for a time refused to believe the evidence of its senses. No man, said the world, could write such undiluted obscurity. The critics approached the borders of delirium trying to discover what it was all about. They failed and consequently either ignored the book or sought to conceal their perplexity under a cloud of witticisms.

To an already sufficiently confused thought the author had added the confusion of the Browningesque manner at its worst confounding. He had started with an assumption of the reader's omniscience and then went on in wild leaps

from one idea to another without stopping to sketch the mental processes that inspired them.

It was too much, even for his friends. Douglas Jerrold made the sad mistake of trying to beguile the tedium of convalescence from a severe illness with Browning's new book. He was quite cheerful, even eager, when he opened the slim volume, but an hour later his wife found him, startlingly pale and staring horribly from among his pillows. She cried out in alarm, but Jerrold was still able to speak.

" It's my mind," she heard him say weakly. " My strength is coming back, but my mind is going. I can't understand the English language any more."

Robert himself grew equally puzzled to remember his meaning, and years later he was obliged to admit when pressed for an interpretation:

" When that poem was written, two knew what it meant — God and Robert Browning. Now God alone knows! "

Tennyson departed from his attitude of admiration to complain:

" I understood only the first line and the last, and both of them are lies."

The first line is:

" Who will, may hear Sordello's story told."
and the last informs all who plod so far:

" Who would has heard Sordello's story told."

Even Elizabeth Barrett's love was only able to manage the doubtful compliment:

"It is a noble picture with its face to the wall just now."

Robert never again attained the incomprehensibility of "Sordello," but his reputation was made forever. It was too late for him to persuade anyone that he meant only what he wrote. The passion for interpreting Browning, for poring over moods and tenses and genders, enveloped every phrase in all his poems until even Pippa's thoughtless little song:

> "God's in his heaven —
> All's right with the world!"

has been discovered as the authentic credo of Robert Browning, philosopher, who selected the song for its very simplicity as suitable to the ignorant child who sang it. His "depressing optimism" was hardly the irritatingly cheerful cry of Pollyanna. He never believed that just because he was happy all the world should be happy with him. And on the rare occasions when he was not happy, he was quite human enough to want the world to be miserable with him.

For some time after "Sordello" appeared, he sought in vain for a publisher for his other poems and a producer for his plays. At last Edward Moxon proposed an experiment. He would print Robert's works in pamphlet form, sixteen pages in double columns of cheap type, the whole edition of each pamphlet to cost only twelve to fifteen pounds —

the author's money, of course. They would be retailed at sixpence the copy. Robert consented, reflecting that he might in this way reach the masses without resorting to magazines. He had already acquired a prejudice against magazines. He felt like an uninvited guest when he thought that careless folk flipping the pages of their favorite journal might suddenly, unexpectedly and perhaps resentfully find him there.

So for five years his works appeared solely in Moxon's pamphlets — except for a couple of short poems contributed to *Hood's Magazine* as a personal favor to help out the dying editor. The price of successive numbers was raised from sixpence to a shilling, then to two shillings and finally to half a crown, but no matter how high it went, the " Bells and Pomegranates," as Robert called the series which contained some of his best poems and worst plays, did not go very fast. For one stretch of six months not a single copy was sold. Still, as Moxon had predicted, the loss was slight.

" Strafford " had not cooled Robert's stage fever. He had two more plays ready for production within a few months after " Sordello's " publication. They were " King Victor and King Charles " and " The Return of the Druses." Macready turned them both down, but he did want a Browning play, and quickly.

Assured of that, Robert went into retirement for five days and came out, weary but triumphant, with " The Blot in the 'Scutcheon." He had conceived his plot, worked it out and put the whole five acts on paper in one extended, exalted surge of poetic frenzy. The piece was destined to become the most often acted of any Browning play, although its literary quality fell far short of " The Druses " or " Luria," both impossible to produce but both rich reading.

Macready accepted the work of the five days at once, but it developed that after all he was not in such a hurry as he had seemed. " The Blot " was written in December, 1841, and not produced until May, 1843. The theme was a little daring; Robert's heroine was actually " a ruined girl." Macready was broad-minded, but unfortunately his determination to uplift the drama had brought him to the verge of bankruptcy, the usual fate of idealists who try to give the public what they think the public ought to like. Macready himself was the only lion in any of his shows, and Queen Victoria saw none of them six times.

His finances were in such a state that he would gladly have returned Robert's manuscript. But he did not like to confess his need and the author misunderstood all hints, even kept pressing impatiently for a production. In a desperate effort at discouragement, Macready had the prompter, " a grotesque person with a red nose and a wooden leg," read the play. The assembled cast, fresh from two failures, had its first good laugh in weeks as the poor man blushed and stammered through the ardent love scenes.

Robert was furious. Macready made amends by reading

the play himself, but explained that it would be impossible for him to take the lead. That would have to be given to Phelps, a minor member of the company. Still Robert did not take the hint. He agreed to Phelps, thinking he was doing his old friend a real favor and not understanding the folly of trying a show in Macready's own theater without Macready. The actor had played his last card. Since to save his pride it was inevitable that the play go on, he would do what he could to save it. He would play the lead after all. But again he misjudged his author. Phelps, miserable at the prospect of losing his chance, appealed to Robert, who insisted that a part once promised could not be taken away.

"I beg pardon, sir, " he told Macready with awful politeness as he rammed his hat firmly and ostentatiously upon his head, "but you have given the part to Mr. Phelps and I am satisfied he should act it."

Despairing of making progress against such stupidity, Macready in a rage hurled the manuscript on the floor and allowed the business to proceed without his aid.

With scenery and costumes drawn rather haphazard from the storehouse and, as Robert complained, "in a miserable, great, chilly house," the play was given to a scant public. There was every reason to believe that the pit would run knee deep in tears at the pathos of the poor, dear heroine's lapse from virtue and her terrible punishment. The lines could almost have been guaranteed to break an audience down. Gags that were to become the favorites of the "ten, twent', thirt'" school of melodrama and were already tried, proven hits in the theater studded the text. There was even the highly affecting moment when the leading lady with downcast eyes and modest mien stepped forward to the footlights and confided shyly:

"I was so young—I had no mother, and I loved him so."

Dickens, who had seen the manuscript, wrote with great feeling to Forster — Robert did not find it out for thirty years and always regretted that the kind message had not been conveyed to him more promptly:

"I know nothing that is so affecting, nothing in any book I have ever read, as Mildred's recurrence to that 'I was so young — I had no mother.'"

But even in 1843 there were a few hard-boiled realists among first-nighters who did not weep so easily as the sentimental Dickens. There were more who regarded with an indignation which they took to be moral any references to the regrettable "facts of life."

"A few of the audience laughed, others were shocked and many applauded," the *Athenaeum* reported tersely.

The reviewer was charitable. The roar of laughter that greeted the opening scene would have doomed any tragedy. For even that exceedingly proper audience saw the joke when the hero, climbing by night into his mistress's bedroom (for no good), sang cheerfully to himself as he climbed:

" There's a woman like a dew-drop; she's so purer than the
purest."

" The Blot in the 'Scutcheon " ran three nights with
only the gallery reasonably well filled. Decidedly it was
too bad Browning wrote those plays. He had lost a friend
by it, for he and Macready could not forgive each other
the failure. Their friendship for all its promising start had
produced only hatred, a half dozen bad plays and " The
Pied Piper of Hamelin," written when little Willy Macready
was sick so that the child might have something to illus-
trate with the crude crayon drawings of his four-year-old
imagination.

But Robert was not easily discouraged. He wrote " Colombe's Birthday " for Charles Kean, who liked it but
wanted to hold it over for a year, keeping it unpublished
meanwhile. As an argument for the delay he explained that
it took him two months to learn a part. This almost disillusioned Robert about the stage, and he wrote bitterly:

" The poorest man of letters (if really of letters) I ever
knew is of far higher talent than the best actor I ever expect
to know."

He refused to withhold publication, and " Colombe's
Birthday " came out in one of Moxon's pamphlets. The
piece, strangely enough, was not a tragedy but the result
was. It was Robert's fate that his plays lost him friends. This
time he quarreled with Forster over the critic's verdict:

"We abominate his tastes as much as we respect his genius."

Robert interpreted this as the superlative of abomination, perhaps with reason. To be accused of bad taste was not to be borne, and the quarrel followed, although years later the two forgave each other.

On the whole it had been an exhausting time. Robert needed rest and went off to Italy to find it. An unfortunate lapse of memory sent him aboard the ship without a morsel of food. Passengers on merchant vessels in the forties were expected to " find " themselves; the owners did not take chances on wasting valuable supplies upon the uncertain landlubbers. So through the long voyage, Robert subsisted on hard, dry biscuits and water, eaten at the sailors' mess. He reached port ravenous, amazingly healthy and proud of the friendship of a rough, good-natured crew who were won by the landsman's eager, uncomplaining participation in their mode of life. They spun him yarns of the sea and he reciprocated with stories nicely calculated to enthrall their imagination, for he always knew just the right kind of tale for any company. The whole adventure, he said, was ample compensation for an unsatisfactory diet.

He saw more of beloved Italy than on his first trip, thanks to a young Neapolitan picked up on the way. His love suffered no diminution, especially as his new friend relieved him of all the necessity for those ferocious financial encoun-

ters which accompanied the payment of every bill. Young
Scotti enjoyed the battle as only a Neapolitan or an Arab
can, and Robert's thrifty instincts were gratified by the
money saved.

His material satisfaction did not interfere with his making
the trip something of a poetic pilgrimage. He haunted the
scenes of Byron's exile, gathering hemlock at the grotto of
Egeria with solemn reverence in the belief that he was pluck-
ing fennel. Later he stood with bowed head beside the grave
of Shelley and was reminded of his youthful admiration.

He came back to England to learn that Elizabeth Barrett
had published a new book. He read and rejoiced, for his
name was bracketed in " Lady Geraldine's Courtship " with
the great of literature. His heart, easily uplifted by the
slightest words of praise, thumped gratefully as he read:

> " . . . . Or from Browning
> Some ' Pomegranate,' which if cut deep
>   down the middle
> Shows a heart within, blood-tinctured,
>   of a veined humanity."

FIVE

LETTER TO A LADY

"M Y cousin is a great invalid and sees no one," Kenyon told the eagerly grateful Robert, "but great souls jump at sympathy."

"If I were to write now?" Robert suggested.

"She would be pleased."

The letter that of course resulted was an enthusiastic expression of gratitude and delight in her verses and ended:

"I love your works, my dear Miss Barrett, and I love you too."

He meant it, and to Dommett he had already written:

"There have come out some divine things by Miss Barrett."

In his letter he had not laid it on too thick. The sick woman wrote joyfully to a friend:

"I had a letter from Browning, the poet, last night which threw me into ecstasies — Browning, the author of 'Paracelsus' and King of the Mystics."

She was nearly forty, she had been an invalid for more than twenty years, but she reacted like a school-

girl to the ardor of her new correspondent. That was
not surprising, for she had never had even a school-girl's
experience.

She believed her real life had ended on the day in her
sixteenth year when she had been thrown from a pony and
hurt her spine. Ever since, she had occupied the fragile and
lonely position of a recognized genius in a large family of
satisfied mediocrity. They were very proud of their Ba;
such a girl was not the possession of every middle-class
merchant household. But they treated her very much as they
did the overly ornate knickknacks on the mantlepiece. Only
Edward, the oldest boy, realized that his sister was actually
human, and she rewarded this brotherly appreciation with
an adoring devotion.

Herself the eldest of eleven children, she had seen but
little of a gentle, harassed, bullied and busy mother who
found her husband more trying than all her children put
together. The poor woman died quite early under the strain
and Edward Barrett Moulton-Barrett superintended the up-
bringing of his children with a sternness so erratic as to
verge on madness. He had three daughters and his opinion
of women was low. When his imagination failed him in the
matter of names for so much offspring, he conferred upon
the two youngest, both boys, the labels of Septimus and
Octavius. Girls did not count in his scheme of things, although in time he derived from the world's recognition of

his daughter's genius the same satisfaction that men of his class find in honors and titles.

Like Bob Browning, he had inherited estates in the West Indies. But Barrett approved of slavery, not only on economic but on moral grounds. He believed sincerely in the essential rightness of the servitude of others. Emancipation of the slaves, which considerably reduced his income and forced him to give up his handsome country estate, Hope End, enraged and embittered him. He would have regarded as heresy, if he had known of it, his daughter's verdict:

" Nevertheless, I am glad, and always shall be, that the negroes are — virtually — free."

So long as his mastery was unquestioned, Barrett was kind to his slaves, more so than most rich men of the day. At Hope End he instructed the poor in piety and literature, and even tried a little at times to improve their material condition, inspiring thereby in his eldest daughter a devotion which no later rough treatment could efface. He was an indulgent parent for the most part, when properly humored, and his maniacal furies when he was crossed insured the humoring.

He tolerated from the first his eldest child's poetic talents. She had begun rhyming before she could talk plainly. As Robert hid his masterpieces under the cushions of an armchair, she, for different reasons, concealed hers beneath the

mattress of her crib. The presence of so many other children in the house kept her from over-indulgence in literature, although she read Homer to her dolls and took her favorite books on long walks to give the poor musty darlings the benefit of fresh air. She also cultivated a garden, collected bugs, developed an exaggerated girlish fear of thunder, led her brothers and sisters in excursions with the over-burdened pony and wrote heroic dramas which were acted in the nursery.

Old Barrett was seized with a temporary fit of broad-mindedness and allowed her, though only a girl, to study Greek with Edward's tutor. About the same time she went through a deliciously daring spell of agnosticism in which she adopted gleefully, and surreptitiously, the old sceptic prayer:

"Oh, God, if there is a God, save my soul, if I have a soul."

But her dissenter's blood was too Puritan for her to maintain such an attitude of revolt against her chapel-going father. Religious doubts were superseded by the prevailing worship of Lord Byron. In common with a million other girls she dreamed passionately of running away to find employment as the poet's page and becoming the adored inspiration of the great lover.

Then, when she was thirteen, she found her father in another indulgent mood. She had written an ambitious epic, "The Battle of Marathon," and he liked it so well that he had fifty copies printed.

Two years later she injured her spine, recovering from the accident only to fall a victim to consumption in the cold London to which the Barretts removed after the financial setback of emancipation.

The London she knew was quite a different place from the gay amusing city in which the young Browning was just finding his way. For her there was only a big, gloomy house in Wimpole Street — "Newgate turned inside out," she called it, and she hated it after the freedom of the country. Though she respected her father, the head keeper of this prison, it was none the less a prison. Her doctors, in the belief that fresh air was bad for her malady, permitted her only occasional excursions outside, and these never took her to those lively, flirtatious regions where fashion and wit helped each other improve the time.

She wrote verses that gained for her the acquaintance of some of the more serious scholarly and literary figures of the day. She published a translation of "Prometheus" and a volume of original poems. Some of these last, kind friends told her, were "harder to interpret than Browning himself."

"Only I cannot believe it," she protested. "He is so very hard."

In the chill damp of the city she found it increasingly painful to breathe, but she refused to mourn her fate. Illness

by this time was an old comrade, and she jested with him although her blue lips sometimes quivered with pain. Finally she grew so weak that Edward insisted on taking her to the milder air of Torquay. He even defied his father by staying longer than was originally intended.

A few days later his drowned body was found on the beach, and his overturned boat, floating emptily under the clear sky, haunted Ba for years. Grief and remorse — for she considered herself the cause of Edward's death — sent her back home so close to death that even her father refrained from uttering any reproaches, although he regarded the whole affair as God's judgment upon filial disobedience. His daughter was pitifully grateful for his forbearance. She was not used to it.

Since then she had scarcely ever left her own room with its books and pictures of her literary idols. They looked down upon her days of pain and sleepless nights. For years sleep "avoided me except in a red hood of poppies," she wrote, explaining that her only relief came from drugs. But in the intervals of suffering she managed at last to go on with her writing. Of one of her poems she was able to say:

"Mr. Horne, the poet, and Mr. Browning, the poet, were not behind in approbation. Mr. Browning is said to be learned in the Greek, especially in the dramatists."

From that time, the learned one's picture hung in her gallery just below that of Wordsworth. A little later she

begged from Kenyon a note which Robert had written and preserved it for the autograph. She found it years later when she had plenty of specimens of her own and she marvelled then at the presentiment which had caused her to write to Kenyon:

"And then Mr. Browning's note! Unless you say 'nay' to me I shall keep this note, which has pleased me so much, yet not more than it ought."

There was little wonder that she went into "ecstasies" over a note of her own. It aroused all her feminine coquetry, never so effective as when sincere. With an astonishing humility she replied by praising "dear Mr. Browning" far more than he deserved and asked gracefully "in the humble low voice which is so excellent a thing in women — particularly when they go a-begging" for criticism of her work.

SIX

AN EPISTOLARY LOVER

T HEY were off to a flying start. Robert accepted the task of mentor, and then regretted loudly and politely the day when he engaged to find faults in her perfect books. He was the ideal critic. Within two weeks Ba was writing to an old friend:

" I am getting deeper and deeper into correspondence with Robert Browning, poet and mystic, and we are growing to be the truest of friends. If I live a little longer shut up in this room, I shall certainly know everybody in the world."

On both sides, however, the first of the letters were rather coy. Neither could forget that this was a correspondence between poets, and both put their art on such a solemnly high level that it seriously hampered their style. But it also made for mutual confidence. Even when Ba complained lightly of Robert's " Sordelloisms " — so she always denominated his obscurities — she knew his heart was right. She could trust any poet of such fervor and sincerity.

Not that they became " Ba " and " Robert " to each other so quickly. For weeks and weeks it was " Dear friend," and

63

then for much longer "Dearest friend." Suddenly, as such things happen, the "friend" disappeared altogether. But in January of 1845 they were still in the formal stage. They might have remained there indefinitely but for Elizabeth Barrett's good sense.

Bullied all her life into accepting in detail all the petty rules of conduct which her father's caste worshipped more rapturously than did that synonym for conventionality, Victoria, she was still able to laugh at the forms she could not help observing. Browning, whose pride was in being the complete gentleman of his time, regarded with horror the slightest lapse from the smallest canon of respectability. But behind his respectability lurked the artist. In the impeccable phraseology of the period, retouched with more than a shade of the Browningesque obscurity, he managed to convey his meaning to a heart that went more than half way to meet his.

Her previous experience of love was worthless here. There had been some tentative advances from a youth who was, she had been told in confidence, paying more ardent court to another lady. Later she was the recipient of mash notes from male admirers of her works who seemed to confuse the poetess with the poems. But these epistles she, with maidenly modesty, burned as quickly as she read. She had been thus repelled by the perfidy of common men, but she was easily stirred by a poet's phrases. Now she did not hesi-

tate to lead the new young man on — in a perfectly nice way, of course.

"*Don't* let us have any constraint, any ceremony," she urged after three weeks of politeness. "*Don't* be civil to me when you feel rude."

The blend of woman's charm with man's freedom of expression was irresistible, as it always is. Not that Robert ever could be rude, perish the thought! But how sweet to know that he might be and still retain Miss Barrett's friendship. He decided to be frank and his reply was:

"I had rather hear from you than see anybody else. *Can* you read this? Because I could write a little better but not so fast."

They were very busy getting acquainted. She demanded to know what he read, what his writing habits were, who started him on his career, whether he had remained true to the tastes and aims of his youth, all about him. He told her of his friends and his regrettable idleness, of his books, his family, his childhood and his hobbies. He enlarged on his headaches — they usually came after he had been dancing all night, but the obvious cause and remedy did not avert Ba's anguished sympathy. She begged him to see a doctor, sleep more, take exercise, travel, abandon the cold showers of which he bragged. Of her own very real sufferings she said nothing.

With rare skill she wrote, not too much, of his work. She

told him of her friends and a little of her life. She confessed to an invalid's passion for romances, the long drawn out three and four volume novels of the day. Both wrote eagerly of the day in spring when warm weather would have restored Ba to enough of health to enable them actually to meet. Meanwhile Robert obeyed her prohibition so literally that he refrained from passing through Wimpole Street when his engagements would normally have taken him there.

He was a scrupulous young man, six years younger than Ba, and already the figure of old Barrett was shadowing their love. Ba's fear of his wrath communicated its uneasiness to her lover. Robert never saw Barrett, but the old man's spirit seemed always with them, and between them. To a violent temper and an exaggerated — even for 1845 — notion of filial duty, Barrett added a mania against matrimony or any friendship which seemed to his suspicious eye to threaten matrimony.

" But if a Prince of Eldorado should come with a pedigree of lineal descent from some signory in the moon in one hand and a ticket of good behavior from the nearest Independent chapel in the other — " Ba had once suggested.

" Why even then," retorted sister Arabel, " it would not *do.*"

They all agreed that it would not do. Edward had wanted to marry and his adoring sister offered to make over to him

her fortune of some £350 a year which had come to her from her father's brother. But Old Barrett, who very much resented the idea of any child of his being independent, brusquely refused to permit the transfer. Later the third sister, Henrietta, had been caught in an innocent affair with a young man and treated to a scene of wild paternal rage which ended only with the erring daughter unconscious on the floor while her trembling, tearful sisters knelt beside her.

There had been nothing as yet between the two poets that even Barrett would have regarded as an avowal. But it was obviously coming, concealed even perhaps from the principals, in a wealth of happy correspondence about the exact meaning of Greek texts, the merits of their contemporaries and the true philosophy of life. Occasionally there was a prophetic reference to her father, and there survives this description of the Barrett household from the loyally indignant pen of Arnould:

" She had been for some years an invalid, leading a very secluded life in a sick-room in the home of one of those tyrannical, arbitrary, puritanical rascals, who go sleekly about the world, canting Calvinism abroad, and acting despotism at home. Under the iron rigor of this man's domestic rule she, feeble and invalided, had grown up to eight and thirty years of age in the most absolute and enforced seclusion from society, cultivating her mind to a wonderful

amount of accomplishment, instructing herself in all languages, reading Chrysostom in the original Greek, and publishing the best metrical translation that has yet appeared of the 'Prometheus Bound'—having also found time to write three volumes of poetry, the last of which raised her name to a place second only to that of Browning and Tennyson amongst all those who are not repelled by eccentricities of external form from penetrating into the soul and quintessential spirit of poetry that quickens the mold into which the poet has cast it. Well, this lady, so gifted, so secluded, so tyrannized over, fell in love with Browning in the spirit before ever she saw him in the flesh — in plain English loved the writer before she knew the man."

But Ba took great pains to explain that she really did love her father, too. He was, she excused him, only a natural born tyrant with certain added idiosyncrasies and a very lonely man — it could not be otherwise for one who held his principles. From time to time he railed at his daughter for eating so little. Obstinacy and a diet of dry toast, he complained, kept her ill; beef and porter would make her well again. Every evening between eleven and twelve he paused on his way to bed to pray with Ba for her soul and her recovery.

From his harshness Robert recoiled as from a ghost; there could be no striking at it; the man was Ba's father. A supposed glimpse of Barrett on the stairs in Wimpole Street

frightened the visitor. But Ba made inquiries and was able to report with some relief:

"No, it was neither father nor other relative of mine, but only an old friend in rather an ill temper."

Despite this constant threat of Barrett's rage — perhaps because of it — the two poets were very happy. Robert wrote of "this old room where I sit all day," but it was a figure of speech, understood as such. For he still went out as much as ever, though he worked a little harder in between. Carlyle was in the throes of his "Cromwell" and Robert was aiding in the research. He was helpful, too, in luring letters of the Lord Protector from suspicious owners. Carlyle's querulous little ways seemed somehow to annoy the possessors of valuable manuscripts, but they yielded easily to Robert's diplomacy.

Also the critics were beginning to notice with increasing annoyance the existence of a poet named Robert Browning. He read their views and took comfort from the memory of Lady Blessington's dictum on a people she knew well:

"The reading world of a certain class account as a personal insult any attempt to instruct them."

Robert dealt, himself, with the reviewers, by writing to Dommett:

"God send I be not too proud of their abuse! For there is no hiding the fact that it is of the proper old drivelling

virulence with which God's Elect have in all ages been regaled."

Robert was certainly not the man to try hiding such a fact. Furthermore he was impersonally enraged by the way the critics were handling young Patmore. They were almost indecent, not because they did not like Patmore's works but because they did not like his father. The elder man was being ostracized by good journalists because, twenty years before, he could have and did not stop a duel in which Scott, editor of the *London Magazine,* was killed. Robert, however, was fond of all the world, except reviewers, just then. Besides, he considered duelling a long established convention and therefore a desirable institution, an opinion he maintained until Ba converted him. So with the best intentions in the world he offered a critic during a ball an introduction to the new writer.

" No," replied the virtuous journalist, " because of that bloody-minded father."

The father was standing near, looking with sad, disillusioned old eyes out over the bulge of his white cravat, " and grateful to me," Robert recorded, " for speaking to ' his boy.' Are not these things fit to make an apostle swear ? "

But in spite of the critics, the editors were becoming more friendly to the author of " Bells and Pomegranates." The young man was acquiring influence and wrote to Dommett

in New Zealand that he could get poems published if Dommett would only write them. He was still violating his principles by permitting some of his best work to appear in *Hood's Magazine,* and other editors were kind to writers who were helping out a dying colleague.

There was respect as well as affection in the glances with which these men greeted Robert now. The young man of fashion was displaying an insight into the minds of men long dead, was recapturing in verse that almost obliterated memories of "Sordello" something of the spirit of past ages. He was developing a poetic form which he was soon to carry to perfection, the dramatic monologue. He had a proper respect, which was lacking in his contemporaries, for his story and a flair for the right kind of story to tell. The "clever person," as he once described himself, could enter into the feelings of men who had lived violently, lustfully, beautifully. He could do more; he could describe their feelings in bursts of language that have never been surpassed. Already he had put into the mouth of David the lines:

> "Then I, as was meet,
> Knelt down to the God of my fathers, and rose on my feet,
> And ran o'er the sand burnt to powder. The tent was un-
> looped;
> I pulled up the spear that obstructed, and under I stooped;

Hands and knees on the slippery grass-patch, all withered
  and gone,
That extends to the second enclosure; I groped my way on
Till I felt where the foldskirts fly open. Then once more I
  prayed,
And opened the foldskirts and entered, and was not afraid
But spoke, 'Here is David, thy servant!' And no voice
  replied.
At the first I saw naught but the blackness — the vast, the
  upright
Main prop which sustains the pavilion: and slow into sight
Grew a figure against it, gigantic and blackest of all.
Then a sunbeam, that burst thro' the tent-roof, showed
  Saul."

As here he caught not only the soul of the time but even
a Biblical sonority of tone and loftiness of language, so in
"The Bishop Orders His Tomb at Saint Praxed's Church"
he expressed, as such a Bishop might actually have done,
a pagan zest for the delights of the senses:

> "And then how I shall lie through centuries,
>   And hear the blessed mutter of the mass,
>   And see God made and eaten all day long,
>   And feel the steady candle flame, and taste
> Good strong thick stupefying incense-smoke!"

Such poems as these inspired Landor to write benevolently of his young friend:

> " Since Chaucer was alive and hale
> No man has walked along our roads with step
> So active, so enquiring eye or tongue
> So varied in discourse."

" I hope more from Robert Browning, for the people of England, than from any living English writer," Carlyle announced.

But Robert was taking a greater interest in the weather that spring than in the people of England. His moods were happy or somber as the days were warm or cold. He greeted the sun with the adoration of a Zoroastrian and prayed for mild winds with the fervor of a transatlantic flyer. For when the last trace of winter was gone, he was to see Ba; she had promised. As the day approached he was all eager confidence, but she betrayed an increasing nervousness. She knew she was not in the least good-looking; she could not forget that she was six years his senior; she had more faith in the written than in the spoken word, and she had more than an invalid's normal timidity in the presence of strange faces.

" There is nothing to see in me, nor to hear in me," she warned Robert. " If my poetry is worth anything in any eye, it is the flower of me . . . the rest of me is nothing but a root fit for the ground and the darkness."

Robert deferentially suggested that he might be permitted to judge that for himself. The flowers were blooming in the garden at New Cross, and he sent his first gift, a yellow rose crushed in a letter. Ba was amused. She had read the Dictionary of Flowers if he had not, and she knew that the yellow rose was the token of infidelity. But it was also a token of summer and a reminder that these serene May days were the time for her to redeem her promise.

"Come Tuesday at three," she wrote at last, and as she penned the words, sudden, inexplicable tears ran down her cheeks.

SEVEN

COURTING

A T three o'clock Robert was gazing curiously upon the front of the tall, narrow, dark house which bore the number "50 Wimpole Street." Unpleasant looking place, he thought it, even as he divided his attention between a last glance at his watch and an effort to control the sudden rush of blood to the head.

Arabel answered his knock. He followed her up the gloomy staircase, staring at Ba's sister with such unseeing eyes that he did not recognize her when they met again. Nor did he hear her polite murmurs as she led the way and threw open to him the gates of Heaven.

It was a Paradise which only his eyes could distinguish. The heavy, dark furniture, the books and papers scattered everywhere, the stained glass window which gave a certain artificial brightness to the room might just as well have been shreds of cloud for all Robert saw of them. He looked only at the slight, plainly dressed figure lying on the sofa.

Long black curls fell on either side of his hostess's pale face and were twisted up into a knot at the back of her head.

Her brown eyes were small and bright. Her nose was rather long, her mouth large. Her dark skirt hung in voluminous folds above many petticoats and completely concealed her feet. The frail body was pinched in at the waist to the point of suffocation, but the fashionable, lady-like hour-glass figure was attained. Her only ornament, the only break in the complete severity of her dress, was a tiny locket at her throat. She was horribly nervous, but the corners of her mouth twisted upwards just a little. They always did; her humor would persist through pain or grief or fear right up to the very moment of complete collapse.

It was a spirit Robert could admire boundlessly. Without any too much spontaneous humor himself, both his good judgment and his sentimentality were captivated by Elizabeth Barrett's unquenchable sense of the ridiculous. He had come expecting to find perfection, and he was always finding what he looked for.

For an hour and a half he sat beside her. Their only chaperon was her little dog, Flush, Kenyon's gift. A little too fat, much too spoiled, but a great comfort in his silent devotion, he gave Ba the only living companionship she had been able to endure for any length of time.

Before she and Robert had exchanged half a dozen sentences, both of them had regained their natural manners. His admiration was so obvious that her nervousness was manifestly out of place. They talked without constraint, and

without excitement either. Occasionally she glanced at a spot on the wall just below Wordsworth's portrait. Robert's picture was no longer there. She had removed it just before he came, but now she was comparing the original with her memory of the picture. It did not do him justice, she decided. Tennyson's portrait was also missing.

" I would not have his hung up and yours away," she confessed later.

She pasted the Browning likeness inside her copy of " Paracelsus," and future visitors wondered why that had suddenly become her favorite book.

This visitor was enjoying himself greatly. He and Ba both liked to talk, and they did it well. Robert knew any number of anecdotes about men she admired, and he relished the telling of them. She could comment charmingly on his stories and express her own opinion in words as perfect as her poems.

She had been afraid before she saw her hero that he had been damaged a little by his life in Society. A man of the world — so she thought of him — how could it be otherwise? She was, therefore, all the more thankful to confess her error.

" Safe and free and calm and pure from the besetting sins of our society," was her report.

The guest departed reluctantly at tea-time. In the street outside he looked at his watch again and jotted down a note

77

—" May 20, 3-4:30." He had become painfully methodical. He kept a minute account of his expenditures, and now, side by side with that record, he began a budget of the minutes spent in Wimpole Street. Every time he called, he carefully noted the exact moment of arrival and departure so that he might treasure up the balance of minutes spent in Heaven. He was much more the bank clerk than was his father.

He hurried home on this May twentieth to spread his raptures on paper. But he was, on second thought, a little apprehensive, too. Did he, he wrote to Ba before he sat down to his dinner, do anything wrong — speak too loud, for instance, a habit which he recognized but never corrected? She reassured him. Nothing had been wrong, she replied emphatically; she could not recall hearing any loud speaking.

She was so full of the visit that she could not refrain from mentioning it to her father. Besides, an apparent frankness was the best means of disarming suspicion.

" It is most extraordinary," she said, " how the idea of Mr. Browning does beset me — I suppose it is not being used to see strangers in some degree — but it haunts me; it is a persecution."

Old Barrett was shocked. Hospitality was a convention to which he paid lip service.

" It is not grateful to your friend to use such a word," he reproved his daughter, and she said no more about it.

The next morning she got another letter. Her assurance that nothing was wrong at their first meeting had emboldened Robert. After two days of contemplating with the absorption of a mystic the passionate intensity of his own emotions, he became reckless. His letter was a mad declaration of love and an insistent proposal of marriage. As a literary masterpiece, Ba thought it beautiful. As a disturbing element in the life of an invalid, it was terrific. She was so deliciously alarmed that she could not sleep at night and lived for days in constant fear that she would become delirious and talk about it.

To Robert, however, she wrote with some measure of forced calm that he was speaking wildly, intemperately, and must never mention such things again. If he did — and she underscored the next line very heavily:

"*I must not — I will not see you again.*"

But she was not cold to his advances. She admitted the beauty of the epistle ("as a dramatic composition") and recognized it as worthy of the poet, saying:

"I do not write as I might of some words of yours — but you know that I am not a stone, even if silent like one."

She advised Robert to burn his letter, which she sent back to him, and he did it. Months later she appreciated her loss and begged to have it returned to her. It was too late, and she bowed to the inevitable, realizing, she said, that it was no more than she deserved for rejecting, even so mildly and inconclusively, the gift of Robert's love.

For three months he observed her prohibition. Their letters and their conversation returned in outward form to the language proper for poets. She remembered that he was " learned in the Greek " and enlisted his learning and poetic skill in revising her translation of " Prometheus." In return she offered to read his proofs and do his copying for him since his headaches were still bothersome. When they met, they talked more of his poems than of her " Prometheus " and not at all of any new work she might be doing.

Once a week he called, carrying flowers from Sis and cakes for Flush, who did not like him. Flush was afraid of trousers, for he was not used to men, and returned Robert's kindest advances with snarls and snaps. He even sank his teeth into Robert's ankles once or twice, but the poet, smiling happily, insisted that it was nothing and gave some excellent advice on the training of dogs by kindness rather than force.

The early summer passed thus innocuously, but they swerved close to forbidden ground when Ba mentioned that her health might force her to go to Italy for the winter. Robert was all enthusiasm. He came to the weekly meetings primed with information about that beloved country. Sitting respectfully on the edge of his chair he talked fervently of following her to the Mediterranean or launched into elo-quent descriptions of places she really must see. He was a

little worried on these occasions that their tête-à-têtes might be interrupted. Ba reassured him — she was always reassuring him, for in his love he was a perfect coward — that his poetry had wrought its wonders upon the Barrett household.

"As you have 'a reputation' and are opined to talk generally in blank verse, it is not likely that there should be much irreverent rushing into this room when you are known to be in it," she wrote.

In the security engendered by "Sordello," they continued to meet until Robert burst out again:

"Let me say now — *this only once* — that I loved you from my soul, and gave you my life, so much of it as you would take, — and all that is *done,* not to be altered now."

Ba protested, a little more faintly this time. She was absorbed just then by the latest of her father's idiosyncrasies. Without offering any reason, he had calmly rejected medical advice that Ba should be sent to Italy for the winter. He did not approve, that was all, and when it was suggested that another winter in England might kill his daughter, he flew into a temper. She told him what the doctor had said, and he branded her with the two most cutting words in his vocabulary, "undutiful" and "rebellious." She protested her dutiful affection, explained that she only wanted some good reason for making the sacrifice of her health to his pleasure. He would give none, because he had none, but she abandoned the trip anyway, unwilling to expose to the old man's

wrath the sister and brother who would have to go with her. The submission was not enough. Barrett considered that his lightest word should never have been questioned. He marked his displeasure by stopping his midnight prayer-meetings in his daughter's room.

All through the painful days of the struggle, Robert hovered about, writing long encouraging notes, urging her to think of herself alone and quite forgetting that he was not to speak of love. He was full of plans and answers to her objections. He pointed out that if they had been fortunate enough to meet and marry years before, and if she had got sick afterwards, " I should be fulfilling 'a pious duty,' I suppose, in enduring what could not be amended — a pattern to good people in not running away."

Again he wrote that all he asked of the world was to be let live and write, and he could do that best with her. When Barrett's refusal was made definite at last, Robert attained the pinnacle of restrained indignation and unrestrained devotion. He proposed to marry Ba, take her away to Pisa and be only a brother to her.

" I would come when you let me," he cried, " and go when you bade me — I would be no more than one of your brothers — 'no more' — that is, instead of getting tomorrow for Saturday (Ba had changed their day of meeting) I should get Saturday as well — two hours for one — when your head ached I should be here. I deliberately choose the realiza-

tion of that dream (of sitting simply by you for an hour every day) rather than any other, excluding you, I am able to form for this world, or any world I know."

" Henceforward," Ba replied by return post, " I am yours for everything but to do you harm."

But first she wanted to regain a little strength. They would have to wait. Meanwhile she proposed a quiet, happy winter of talk and letters and proof correcting. He might even come twice a week some weeks. Robert bowed to her decision. It was more than he really expected, and he went about the world with the peculiarly annoying happiness of a man very much and very successfully in love. He was seen until dawn at some of the best parties of the season, having a splendid time. He would get home just in time for breakfast, perhaps to find a note from Ba to soothe him. Then he would sit down to tell her before he slept what an inexpressible bore the affair of last night had been. She thought it nice of him to say so, but she didn't believe him.

She was herself in an even worse state than he. She read Mr. Dumas's new book, "The Count of Monte Cristo," and confessed that she got the hero all mixed up with Robert. Thinking of her lover's excellences, she quite lost the thread of the story, but reported that it was a noble book anyway. Again, right in the midst of a choice bit of gossip about Isidore, the Queen's hairdresser and " the most literary man at Court," she fell into a reverie of love. The

story of Isidore passed right over her head, and she did not even regret it.

Robert's letters usually came to her by the post that reached Wimpole Street at eight o'clock, "while all the world is at dinner." Quite alone with her books and her dry toast and Flush, Ba could hear the postman eight or ten doors off, the knockers banging louder and louder as he drew nearer. Every evening she experienced the same thrill; would there be a knock for number 50? There would. A moment later the faithful Arabel slipped upstairs with the letter and a wicked smile.

The letters were in a way so much better than the visits now. Not a word of love was spoken when they were together. In fact they no longer said much of anything, but merely sat and stared and thought. At last, his time up, Robert would rush off home to put down on paper the burning words he had been afraid to speak. The fire might go out and the room get cold, but he would write madly on until called insistently to come down stairs to dinner.

In the state of his emotions, it was perhaps not surprising that his sentences sometimes hardly made good sense. Both lovers analyzed their feelings *in extenso* with the inevitable result that they got beyond the limits even of their vocabularies and were plunged into charming (for them) disputes as to who loved who the most. Robert was always crying out that he was always wrong and she was always right, but

she had just this once a little misapprehended him. What
he had really meant was — and there would follow, and
at length, an explanation sure to mean nothing. Ba would
reply that no, no, he was quite perfect, but at the same time
she did not misunderstand. She had not thought he meant
what he thought she thought he meant and she would proceed to confuse the thought still more. It was no wonder he
had headaches.

There was, for example, the matter of an ivory penholder.
Ba had one that was too heavy for her and she offered it to
Robert so that he should think of her once in a while as he
wrote. The offer, besides filling him with a gratitude out
of all proportion to the gift, induced some reflections which
he expressed thus:

"I woke — late or early — and in one of those lucid moments when all things are thoroughly *perceived,* — whether
suggested by some forgotten passage in the past sleep itself,
I don't know — but I seem to *apprehend,* comprehend entirely, for the first time, what would happen if I lost you —
the whole sense of that *closed door* of Caterina's came on
me at once, and it was *I* who said — not as quoting or adapt-
ing another's words, but spontaneously, unavoidably, ' *In
that door you will not enter, I have* ' . . . And, dearest, the
"Unwritten it must remain.

"What is on the other leaf, no ill omen after all, — because I strengthened myself against a merely imaginary

85

evil — as I do always; and *thus* — I know I can never lose you, — you surely are more mine, there is less for the future to give or take away than in the ordinary cases, where so much less is known, explained, possessed as with us. Understand for me my dearest. — "

To which after speaking in praise of his poetry she replied:

" In the meanwhile you have 'lucid moments,' and strengthen yourself into the wisdom of learning to love me — and upon consideration, it does not seem so hard after all — there is 'less for the future to take away' than you had supposed — so *that* is the way? Ah, 'these lucid moments, in which all things are thoroughly perceived;' what harm they do me! — And I am to 'understand for you,' you say! — Am I?

" On the other side and to make the good omen complete, I remembered, after I had sealed my last letter, having made a confusion between the ivory and horn gates, the gates of false and true visions, as I am apt to do — and my penholder belongs to the wrong gate, — as you will perceive in your lucid moments — poor holder! "

And Robert, after crying out against " perverse interpretations," wound up with:

" And if at any future moment I should again be visited — as I earnestly desire may never be the case — with a sudden consciousness of the entire inutility of all earthly love (since of *my* love) to hold its object back from the decree

of God, if such should call it away; one of those known facts which, for practical good, we treat as supremely common-place, but which, like those of the uncertainty of life — the very existence of God, I may say — if they were *not* common-place; and would they be thoroughly apprehended (except in the chance minutes which make one grow old, not the mere years) — the business of the world would cease; but when you find Chaucer's graver at his work of ' graving smale seles ' by the sun's light, you know that the sun's self could not have been created on that day — do you ' understand ' that, Ba? "

Ba ended this particular exchange by writing:

" Ever dearest, you could not think me earnest in that letter? It was because I understood you so perfectly that I felt at liberty for the jesting a little — for had I not thought of *that* before, myself, and was I not reproved for speaking of it, when I said that I was content for my part even *so*? Surely you remember — and I should not have said it if I had not felt with you, felt and known that ' there is, with us, less for the future to give or take away than in the ordinary cases.' So much less!"

By modern standards they starved their love cruelly. A handclasp was beyond all Robert's daring. A kiss was something mentioned in poetry but never attempted in real life. However, they derived a certain pleasure from the realization that their love could thrive on a diet of mere words.

And of words they were prodigal indeed. Over the exchange of a lock of hair, they lavished enough of ingenuity and lyrical expression to have made a trunkful of the kind of plays Robert wrote. His letter suggesting that she trust him with a wisp of black curl was a masterpiece of dignified pleading worthy of a request for a couple of dukedoms and a principality. He felt greatly daring, and well he might. An admirer of Ba's poetry had only three weeks before made a similar, though not so eloquently phrased plea.

"I am too great a prude for such a thing," she had answered.

But Robert was Robert and should have the great token of confidence — "Oh, you who have your way in everything!" Only he should not ask for it tomorrow. Some day she would slip it into his hand, if he would first give her a lock of his hair to wear in the locket at her throat. And one day she did. Her fingers trembled so much at her shameless conduct that she quite spoiled two locks trying to tie them up with a bit of silk. She was rewarded by Robert's grateful cry:

"I will live and die with your beautiful, your beloved hair — comforting me, blessing me."

As the autumn days grew shorter and gloomier, Ba resorted to little stratagems to delay Robert's departures. She deliberately invited suspicion by sitting with him in the dusk, for she feared he might take the lighting of the lamp

ELIZABETH BARRETT BROWNING

" Nothing of that peculiarity which one would expect from reading her poems."

as a signal to go. Alas, he remained fully aware of the flight of time and left at the usual hour.

He was a very discreet young man. One night at Talfourd's, whither Ba's lawyer brother, George, had gone for the sole purpose of watching the author of "Paracelsus" with his inimitable grace hopping a sedate and stately Polka, Robert exercised his discretion by inquiring with a polite indifference, which he found most difficult to assume, how Miss Barrett did. George, who had seen the poet leaving Wimpole Street a couple of hours before, chuckled and said, "Quite well." But he told Ba he had found Robert "unassuming," and admired him as much as if he had been a lawyer. Robert was gratified, for he had put himself out to be nice to George, "meaning to get a friend in him."

The visit of which George had seen the end marked for Robert another stage in the mathematical progress of his romance. He indulged in a few minutes of arithmetic that night and was able to announce that he and Ba had now spent just forty-eight hours in each other's company. It was what he called a great fact, considering that every time he called he resolved to go sooner and departed regretting that he had not stayed longer. Ba was not impressed.

"So little!" she exclaimed when she saw his figures. She was never one to measure her emotions by the clock.

She did contrast her lover with Henrietta's new young man, and found every reason to be complacent. Captain

Surtees Cook was as different from Robert as a man could be. He was a distant cousin of the Barretts, and he used his privileged position to oust two rivals. His methods did not appeal to Ba. He called determinedly, when the head of the house was out, every day. He proposed once a week and was rejected with equal regularity. On each of the other six days he spent four hours treating Miss Barrett to a series of the most unsoldierly displays — " the whole house heard his fits of hysterical sobbing," Ba said disgustedly. Poor Henrietta did not have her sister's strength of mind. She capitulated at last, and thoroughly. The household, no longer bored by the Captain's tearful outbursts, was condemned to listen to Henrietta's confidential eulogies of the excellent qualities she was discovering in him.

All unconscious of the revolt spreading through his domains, old Barrett went calmly about his business. Once or twice, coming home early, he glanced into Ba's room and saw Robert sitting there. He was not disturbed. It was only " Mr. Browning, the poet — the man of the pomegranates." Mr. Barrett, withdrawing quietly, wondered if the young man talked as queerly as people said he wrote, but he did not attempt to find out.

If he thought about his daughter's health he gave no sign. But he may well have felt a desire to go about saying, " I told you so." For London was enjoying its mildest winter and Ba her best health in many years. She was even able to

walk downstairs on a fine afternoon. She attributed it all to
the effects of love, and enshrined her memory of that time
in the lines:

> "I yield the grave for thy sake and exchange
> My near sweet view of heaven for earth with thee!"

Robert's chief fear concerning her father was that some
day he might seek out the visitor and thank him for the
visits. Robert did not know whether he would be able to
maintain his composure in such a situation. Ba ridiculed the
idea. The situation could not arise. Thanks, she said, were
the last thing her father ever thought of.

She was more worried about Kenyon. That old friend
always talked to her now of Robert and looked at her very
sharply as he talked. She was not good at dissembling, and
his suspicions annoyed her. Once he actually came while
Robert was in the room, but the younger man saved the
day with a barrage of his best anecdotes and his finest society
manner. Her brothers, too, were beginning to wink teas-
ingly, but they knew better than to start anything with their
father. Though Henrietta and Arabel were openly sympathetic, the nervous strain grew worse. Ba was glad she
saw so little of her father. Every footstep frightened her;
every knock except the postman's made her tremble. By the
time spring came again she was in such low spirits that she
wrote:

"It would have been better for you never to have seen my face perhaps."

"Oh, dearest," was Robert's anguished reply, "let us marry soon, very soon, and end all this."

His own family was perfect. They asked no questions. They listened while he talked of Ba. They kept his secret. They only smiled a little when he dragged up to his room the biggest and most comfortable chair he could find and placed it in just the position of Ba's sofa by her own fire. With a volume of her poems in his hand, he would gaze at the empty chair until he had evoked her image. Then he would write her another long letter.

He was seeing good omens everywhere. The *Quarterly* carried a review of their works in one article. That was to him a symbol of their coming marriage. For once in his life he spoke of a critic without using impolite adjectives. He amused himself by picking out a book with his eyes shut and seeking his fortune inside. His mind misgave him when he found an Italian grammar in his hand, but when he opened it he knew that there was a God. For his eyes fell upon an exercise to be translated into Italian and he read:

"If we love in the other world as we do in this, I shall love thee to eternity."

By spring it was evident that Ba was going to be strong enough to run away at the end of the summer. As early as May she went for a drive, actually walked on the lawns at

Regent's Park and found it "the strangest feeling!" She came home to find that Mr. Poe in New York, "whose wild eyes flashed through tears" as he read her verses, had referred to her in a dedication of his own works as "the noblest of your sex." She wondered whether she should not reply: "Sir, you are the most discerning of yours."

She was more interested, however, in the gossip she was hearing about Robert. Twice within a week she was told stories of his love affairs with other women, but even rumor itself was unable to penetrate the armor of the poet's respectability. Every story was exceedingly proper and ended in a betrothal. One woman came all the way from Leeds, apparently for no other reason than to tell Ba that the poet Browning, of whom she must have heard, had once been engaged, but the lady broke it off because of religious differences and married another man. A few days later Arabel brought from the dinner-table a report that the Mr. Browning "of the great genius" was even then engaged to Miss Campbell, the Scotch heiress. Ba only laughed at these tales, but Robert was a little rueful. He would have preferred to cut a more dashing figure in the world of romance.

"They used to get up better stories of Lord Byron," he complained.

However, he did not look so much like the young poet as he had when Macready first set eyes upon him. He was a

shade bulkier in figure and much quieter in dress. Besides, as his biographer, Mrs. Orr, has pointed out:

" Mr. Browning was now engaged to be married and the last ring of youthful levity had disappeared from his tone."

The wedding had been definitely fixed for the autumn. Ba and Robert sent each other books and travelers' letters dealing with the weather in Italian towns, the state of the roads, the food, the quality of the inns, the exposure to tourists. But Ba was still oppressed with occasional qualms that it was too good to last. She worried about Robert's future happiness when he should find what life with an invalid really meant. Robert was defying the world to call him a fortune-hunter, and Ba assured him that " people are more likely to say that I have taken you in." But at last, in her perplexity, she hit upon a solution that marked the only real breach with the conventions that either of them ever contemplated in all their lives. She proposed a trial marriage. They would go off together, legally tied of course, in the fall. But if at winter's end he were tired of the arrangement, she would leave him, taking only so much of her own money as would support her alone in Greece.

" I believe," she explained, " that I never could quarrel with you; but the same cause would absolutely hinder my living with you if you did not love me. We could not live the abominable lives of married people all round — you *know* we could not."

A few weeks before he had exclaimed, paraphrasing Voltaire: "If marriage did not exist, I should infallibly invent it." But now he said:

"Ba, there is nothing in your letter that shocks me — nothing. If you choose to imagine that 'possibility' you are consistent in imagining the proper step to take — it is all imagining. But I feel altogether as you feel about the horribleness of married friends, mutual esteemers, etc."

His poetic strain was becoming more and more pronounced, although it descended upon him only in streaks. He would on one day vow that life could hold no higher happiness than to spend it in a garret with Ba, even if it were a one-room garret. The next day, in a soberer moment, he was discussing the realities of their life together.

"I shall begin," he warned her, "by begging a separate room from yours — I could never brush my hair and wash my face, I do think, before my own father. I could not, I am sure, take off my coat before you *now* — why should I ever?"

Ba did not reply to this plea for privacy, although as one of a large family she appreciated the blessings of a room of her own. But she was wholly occupied just now in trying not to betray her happiness and her fear for another few weeks. It was very hard. Her father thought her "mumpish" and complained severely of her obstinacy. He was even more displeased to find that "the man of the pomegranates" had been with his daughter all one day. There had been a suc-

cession of thunder storms and Ba had an unreasoning terror of thunder. So Robert, who had come earlier than usual and had the good excuse of not desiring a wetting, stayed on and on. Barrett, when he heard of it, looked " as if the thunder had passed into him."

" It appears, Ba," he scolded, " that *that man* has spent the whole day with you."

He was very angry. He went out to explain himself at greater length to Arabel, and Ba, still shivering after the narrowness of her escape from collapse and complete confession, could hear him in the hall roaring about the impropriety of leaving her alone with a man! What if she had been taken ill? he demanded. It would have disgraced the family.

Such scenes as this so shattered her nerves that towards the end of August the realization that his future wife was not in the best of health for a long voyage suddenly dawned upon Robert with all its meaning for the first time. He had been very solicitous but, never having been sick himself, he had not really given the problem much thought. Now he did, and he suggested that they delay no more than a month. Otherwise they would miss the best travelling weather. Ba, as usual, was ready to meet him more than half way.

She asked only a week's notice, for, she wrote, " I felt myself ready to give up the whole world for you at the holding up of a finger."

EIGHT

WAYS AND MEANS

OFTEN, as Robert sat in his room gazing at the empty chair by the fire, he thought more of money than of poetry. He found almost as much pleasure in scheming out ways of earning a living as he did in telling Ba how much he loved her. He never had earned a living — for that matter he never did in all his life make as much as he spent — and the prospect of seeking gainful employment had all the charms of novelty.

His plans were rather wild. At times he even had visions of supporting a family with his pen, but that was only in his most extravagant moods. For the most part he realized that there would have to be a supplementary occupation, and he was ready to give up poetry in exchange for marital comfort, although Ba refused to hear of such a sacrifice. The old flame, Law, no longer held out any charms to him, although acquaintances at the Inns of Court urged him that it was not too late at thirty-four to begin studying for the bar. Diplomacy still beckoned alluringly, and he had moments

in which he ranted, somewhat fantastically, about the solid satisfactions of manual labor.

He wrote to Ba that he could live happily with her on bread and potatoes, that he could groom a horse and would rather do it than be Solicitor-General. He professed a great scorn for Solicitors-General; it seemed the poetic thing to do.

In his mercenary dreams, his faith in the drama revived. Charles Kean had offered him the unheard of price of £500 for a suitable play, and Robert was sure he could satisfy the actor. Colburn, the publisher, was looking for a novel about Napoleon. Robert had never tried that form of literature, but he was sure he could do it. Ba could not quite understand this preoccupation with money matters. She agreed with him that a life of poverty would be a life of happiness if they shared it, but there was no reason for supposing that they would have to. She reminded him that she had enough for both.

" Between us two," she chided, " there can be no worldly considerations."

Robert was a little dashed.

" I alluded to them," he confessed, " rather ostentatiously because — because *that would be* the *one* poor sacrifice I could make you."

So he clung to the subject, insisting he could get rich if he tried.

" Besides what you have thought *genius* in me is certainly

talent, what the world recognizes as such," he informed her.

She did not care to argue that point. Also she could not but respect to a degree his fine scruples against living on her money. So she contented herself with assuring him that they would not have to tell anyone where their money came from. No one, she repeated, would call him a fortune-hunter for £350 a year.

But he went right on making plans. A little calm reflection — he always had these periods of sanity after moments of wildness — brought the realization that they would never be able to live on the proceeds of what he wrote, although the idea was never permanently abandoned. He had also given up the prospect of honest toil. But Lord Monteagle was rising for a brief progress across the political heavens that were being darkened by the mighty fall of Peel, a fall so devastating that Ba and Robert were probably the only two literate persons in all London who never discussed the Corn Laws or Protection or the diabolic cleverness with which " the Hebrew juggler," Disraeli, was overturning the symbol of British solidity. My Lord Monteagle liked Browning's verses and was expected to be a member of the next Ministry. Robert proposed to go to him with the simple plea:

" Will you give me for my utmost services about as much as you give Tennyson for nothing? "

Peel had, a few months before, granted the future Laure-

ate, who was then in poor health, a pension of £200 a year. Robert proposed to earn in the diplomatic service the allowance he hoped to get. He urged Ba to give her annuity to her brothers and sisters immediately, but cannily suggested " a proper reservation in the case of my own exertions failing, as failure comes everywhere." Ba upset that bright dream with a very few words. An unconditional literary pension would be impossible for him to get — he was not sufficiently popular — and what if a diplomatic career were to carry him to a country in which she could not live?

Robert gave up one more idea quite cheerfully, admitted his error and proceeded to evolve another literary scheme. He thought, and backed it up with sound figuring, that by taking to the magazines and similar hack literary fields he would be able to sell his works well enough to make fifty or sixty pounds a year. This, he said with all a lover's lyrical disregard for facts, would be ample for them to live on at Ravenna " with the pines and the sea and Dante and *no* English and all Ba."

He got the notion of this sales value of poetry from a unique literary adventure which had just befallen Ba. A New York publisher who had put out an American edition of her works had actually paid her ten per cent. of all the profits. Her share was fourteen pounds. It was an amazing performance, for it was more than the same works had earned in England, and the absence of an effective inter-

national copyright law permitted unrestricted theft of any foreign writings that pleased a publisher's taste.

"One's poetry," Ba bragged, "has a real 'commercial value' if you do but take it far enough away from the 'civilization of Europe.' When you get near the backwoods and the red Indians it turns out to be nearly as good for something as cabbages."

"America with its ten per cent.," replied Robert, "shall have my better word henceforth and forever, for when you calculate, there must have been a really extraordinary circulation; and in a few months; it is what newspapers call 'a great fact.'"

The publisher's unprecedented generosity towards a mere author was partially explained by a later request that she prepare for the American market some essays she had written in the *Athenaeum*. She did not relish the idea — she was not proud of her prose — but Robert urged her to the work since the offer was a "good, straightforward, un-American thing." As a friend of Dickens, Robert had heard more harrowing tales of literary crime in America than she could dream of, and he warned her not to lay herself open to such treatment as other English writers had to stand. Even Dickens himself had seen his works appear in New York, badly garbled and padded out with page after page of Thackeray's "Yellowplush Papers."

Nevertheless, Ba's experience caused Robert to sing hymns

in praise of America's improved literary taste. His own poems were also being read across the Atlantic and although they produced no munificent sum like fourteen pounds, there was a sturdy satisfaction in knowing that one's works were serving their high purpose among the heathen. In England there was no improvement in the reception accorded by what he was beginning to think of as the " British public, ye who like me not." The last number of " Bells and Pomegranates," the drama " Luria," appeared, enhancing Robert's literary reputation but no whit relieving the burden upon his father's salary. Neither of them thought it at all unnatural that a healthy young man of thirty-four should be dependent even for his most trifling expenditures upon his father. Poetry was a luxury the elder Browning was only too pleased to pay for generously. He paid even more in kindness and sympathy than in money.

"At night," Robert wrote, " he sits studying my works — illustrating them — and yesterday I picked up a crumpled bit of paper, ' his notion of what a criticism on this last number ought to be — none that have appeared satisfying him! ' "

It was a somewhat mournful pleasure he derived from subsidizing and encouraging his son's genius. His hair and beard were almost white now, and behind the cheerful cast of the full, handsome old face there lurked a wistfulness born of nearly forty years at an occupation he detested. On some of these nights as he sat illustrating Robert's poems, his

thoughts were more on what those illustrations might have been than on what the poems were. Loyally he told himself that if life were to be had all over again he would change nothing, nothing. But his drawings sometimes drooped a little, very different from the gay, quirky pieces he sketched for children. With children he was always happy for they adored him with his stories and his caricatures and his sweets. His kindness remained unfailing. Robert, contrasting, perhaps unconsciously, his parent with old Barrett, remarked that no member of the Browning family could express a desire for some trifle but that Bob was on his feet, reaching for his hat, explaining that he had just been wanting to go out and was only looking for an excuse.

From him Robert had never been shy of taking money. But he knew that Bank of England salaries would not maintain two establishments. So when he talked to Ba of their future journeyings, he dwelt at such length on the frugal advantages of using freighters (they were not only cheap but so much more the life of the sea than flash passenger vessels) that she inquired rather timidly if she might be permitted to take her maid, Wilson, with her to Italy.

Wilson, without whose devotion Ba would have lost what meager comforts she found in life, was a very expensive servant. She got sixteen pounds a year in addition to her keep. Like her mistress, she was no longer young and had never been any prettier. One of those small wiry creatures

of rabbity appearance so obviously fitted to wait upon more fortunate women that it never occurs to anyone to consider the tragedy of their servile lives, Wilson expended upon Ba the suppressed affection of a starved and frustrated soul. She defended her mistress from the intrusion of strangers and the excitements of a large household. She posted the letters that went to Robert in a steady stream, and she kept Barrett in ignorance of the magnitude of the correspondence. Robert was just as horrified at the thought of being alone with an invalid wife as Ba was of leaving Wilson to brave the furies of Barrett before being turned out into the street. It would be rank insanity, he exclaimed, to attempt any elopement without Wilson. He shuddered, and underscored heavily as he wrote very firmly on this point. It was nothing that poetry or philosophy could touch. It was a matter of material well-being and essential to happiness. Sixteen pounds a year were at once added to the new Italian budget.

But if Ba was luxurious in the matter of personal attendance, she made up for it by the simplicity of her personal appearance. Her greatest expense was morphine, and she hoped to be able to dispense with drugs in Italy. Never in all her life had she spent more than twenty pounds a year on clothes. The plain, voluminous dark gowns she wore were built to last. The lacy, elaborate negligées of more coquettish invalids never formed part of her desires. She did not venture from the house often enough to wear out either her very sensible shoes or her very modest bonnets. She would have been ashamed to adorn her legs with silk stockings, even although they would have been quite invisible. Her only luxury was losing handkerchiefs with great regularity.

Robert prided himself upon his practical common sense, but it was Ba who wrote out their marriage settlement. This was a curious document, a recognition of his scruples and a determination to take care of him in spite of them. It read:

"In compliance with the request of Robert Browning, who may possibly become my husband, that I would express in writing my wishes respecting the ultimate disposal of whatever property I possess at this time, whether in the funds or elsewhere . . . I here declare my wishes to be — that he, Robert Browning . . . having, of course, as it is his right to do, first held and used the property in question for the term of his natural life . . . should bequeath the same, by an equal division, to my two sisters, or in case of the previous death of either or both of them, to such of my surviving brothers as most shall need it by the judgment of my eldest surviving brother.

ELIZABETH BARRETT BARRETT

Wimpole Street, July, 1846."

They had never discussed the possibility of having an heir of their own. Engaged couples in those days did not mention such indelicate subjects, but this pair never even thought of it. They would have regarded as a painful and indecent jest any suggestion that Ba might ever bear children.

Robert approved her marriage document, and she may have thought it necessary, for the time came when he so entirely reversed his earlier position as to write, a little savagely:

"After my death, I return nothing to your family, be assured."

In the end he always came around to Ba's way of thinking, and now it was she who took up the burden of financial planning. She reported that she thought she could make more money out of her poetry than he from his, a fact about which there could be no difference of opinion. She had been asked to contribute to *Blackwood's Magazine* and figured on a literary income of £100 a year from the reviews and from ballads "for Angus Fife to civilize Australia with." She had another bright idea, too. Kenyon had taken her, on one of her rare excursions into the world, to see the Great Western train come roaring into its station, a new and fashionable sight. The noisy monster, so dirtily prophetic of that progress of which Robert and Ba were the respectable minstrels, had made her head spin and she grew weak contemplating the man-made power of the puffy, arrogant, tin pot locomotive. It also caused her to think of future possibilities.

"When we are free," she wrote, "we ought to place our

money somewhere on the railroads where the percentage will be better — which will not disturb the simplicity of our way of life, you know, though it will give us more liberty in living."

She did not always talk of money and love. She could not praise highly enough the poems and dramas he brought her, but when he asked about her own work she was a little reticent.

"You shall see some day at Pisa what I will not show you now," she said, for she was already embodying in verse the story of their romance.

Robert's indignation against Wordsworth, which culminated in "The Lost Leader," was not shared in Wimpole Street.

"Won't the court laurel (such as it is) be all the worthier of you for Wordsworth's having worn it first?" Ba asked with a touching faith in the intelligence of those who bestow such laurels.

The Laureate did not need her championship. His tongue was far sharper than his pen, and he took care that the younger poet should hear his remarks. Differences of political opinion, he felt, did not call for poetic insults and his early admiration for "the boy" went a little sour. Walking with a friend in Surrey one day, Wordsworth was informed with proper respect that Robert Browning lived over by that hill.

"Hill?" questioned the old man suavely and with the proper emphasis on the more important part of his informant's statement. "We call that, such as that, a rise."

Ba tried to interest Robert in romances, but he remained indifferent to the lure of fiction. He knew so many stranger stories in history, and his matter of fact spirit refused to join her in crying out against Dumas for hanging his hero in Volume Four. Ba was all for forming a "Society for the Prevention of Cruelty to Romance Readers," but Robert thought they deserved whatever they got. He believed this attitude was scientific; he rather prided himself on being scientific. When Occy Barrett was thought to have typhoid fever and Ba warned her lover to stay away from Wimpole Street, he wrote:

"I disbelieve altogether in contagion from fevers, especially typhus fevers — as do much better informed men than myself."

But Occy did not have typhoid, so the visits were not interrupted, although Ba had said:

"I should not trust to your theories — no indeed."

As her own health improved she visited a few old friends and even went to church once. That ordeal was too much for her. The crowd of orderly parishioners terrified her, she was not accustomed to humanity in bulk, and she had to be taken home before the sermon began. Something of the same feeling led to her refusal to drive out to New Cross to see

the Brownings. She was afraid, despite the loving messages
Robert carried to Wimpole Street, and she excused herself
by saying she could not expose them to her father's wrath
after the marriage. Old Barrett was a convenient pretext, but
in reality the qualms and doubts she had felt before allowing
Robert to call assailed her with increased force — for they
were not combatted by love or curiosity — at the prospect
of exhibiting herself, nervous, plain, ill, tougue-tied and
forty, to her lover's family.

Meanwhile she was badly in need of Robert's worldly
advice. The painter Haydon, " poor Haydon," all his friends
called him, removed himself from a world that repaid the
best efforts of his genius with cruelty and contempt. His
paintings were much admired; his lectures on art were
highly praised; he had once numbered among his friends
such men as Peel and Count D'Orsay and Talfourd. But he
had spent many months in debtors' prisons and all the rest
of his life in squalid poverty. A man in whom the domestic
virtues were strong, the sufferings of his large family un-
settled a never too well balanced mind. In an age when
artists needed patrons, Haydon alterately fawned upon and
bullied men of wealth. They found him equally objectionable whether he cringed or boasted. There was only one revenge for the embittered man. He wrote out his memoirs,
a twenty-six volume flood of abuse, calumny and rage. Then
he made a will appointing Elizabeth Barrett his literary

executor and with that last gesture of hatred for mankind blew out his brains.

The interminable mass of his manuscript was duly brought to Wimpole Street. Ba was almost frantic. She had never felt so strongly her detachment from the world, her ignorance of men and women, as now when she read on and on through the mad painter's twenty-six volumes of vituperation and outraged vanity. Poor Haydon had a style, and his impassioned invective was of the kind that leaves its mark wherever it strikes. There was, Ba found, so much personal bitterness, so much that would undoubtedly cause scandal. And yet the task of seeing the books through the press had been laid upon her by a dying man. What, she asked the practical Robert, ought she to do? She thought three volumes might be extracted from the twenty-six, but she was not sufficiently acquainted with the people involved to do the electing. Her judgment, however, proved sound. When, seven years later, Tom Taylor undertook the task he made just three volumes out of Haydon's memoirs.

Robert promptly bestirred himself to be of help. In his world there was now much sympathy for poor Haydon. It would be a shame to alienate this from his unfortunate family by untimely and unkind revelations. Robert discovered that the painter, shrewd in his fierce madness, had selected Ba as his editor just because she knew so little of the world. He had hoped that in her ignorance she would publish all

the indiscretions that anyone of sounder judgment would suppress. So Robert's advice, the counsel of a man who knew his world, was that she should do nothing.

Indeed, it was very easy to forget poor Haydon and his sordid tragedies. Summer was ending, the time when Robert was to claim his bride if she were strong enough was near, and not in many years had she been so well. She walked on the grass more often now and even plucked forbidden flowers (for Robert) in the Botanical Garden while Arabel, holding her skirts wide to shield the culprit from a gardener in the offing (they served some purpose, those gowns of long ago), delivered a lecture on the impropriety of such thieving. There was no reason for further delay, and Robert, writing to friend Dommett in New Zealand about the middle of July, hinted mysteriously:

"I have some important objects in view with respect to my future life — which I will acquaint you with next time I write, when they will be proved attainable or no."

But it was nearly thirty years before he wrote again to the man who sat for the portrait of "Waring," of whom he wrote:

> "Meantime, how much I loved him,
> I find out now I've lost him.
> I who cared not if I moved him,
> Who could so carelessly accost him,

Henceforth never shall get free
Of his ghostly company."

Just now events were moving much too rapidly for writing letters to any but one. The good looking, sober, respectable, cautious young man, the scholar, dancer, fashionable dinner-guest, was being cast in the exacting rôle of a hero of Romance. For once, and for once only, Robert Browning rose above his common sense and his prejudices, and played the part adequately.

NINE

BELLS

T HE end of August found Robert suddenly pressing for an elopement within a month. It would never do to miss good travelling weather, and they had already waited long enough. Ba agreed. She urged him to come to their next meeting prepared to discuss what books should be taken along and how many. But somehow they never got around to that subject and had to decide by letter not to take any books at all.

There was so much to be done that Robert hardly had a chance to think. He ran madly about the town seeking information concerning boats, inquiring of his friends what they knew of roads and inns in Italy. Should one go to Ravenna or Pisa or Rome or one of the innumerable little resorts of which one knew nothing? He wavered between a consuming desire to be quite alone with his beloved and an intense fear that such solitude might prove too much for her. He did not dare ask Ba directly, for that would be to doubt her love, but he managed to pack a quantity of facts about Italy into his daily letters in the hope that she would, unasked, express a preference.

She did not, for she was having her own troubles. Flush was stolen from under the wheels of her carriage, right in front of her house, and she worried about the poor little creature's terrors, for he was no more used to the world than she. But she was wise in the ways of "the banditti" who made their living out of women's pets. Flush had been stolen before, and every dog owner in London could have told her how to go about getting him back. The business was well organized and lucrative for the section of the underworld that went in for canine kidnapping. They netted from three to four thousand pounds a year in ransoms.

Brother Henry volunteered to conduct the negotiations for Flush's return and hurried down to the recognized dog exchange. But business was not done so quickly there. The gang knew the cash value of suspense and liked to proceed at their leisure. Henry came home empty-handed and angry. He was visited that night by one Taylor, chief negotiator of the confederacy, a cheerful braggart who had kept his hat on in some of the best houses in town and always had an opulent cigar glued to the corner of his mouth. The pup, he announced, was quite safe in Whitechapel. Henry would be notified as soon as Taylor's board of directors had fixed the price. Henry longed to make a few threatening, futile re-

marks about the police and prison, but Ba insisted that he treat the visitor with respect.

Robert was fiercely indignant. He declared that he would have informed the villain to return the dog by morning or he, Robert, would spend the rest of his life hounding the thieves to their destruction. Ba did not think all of them put together were worth one hair from Flush's silky ears. She wanted her pet, not the lives of his kidnappers. Despite her anguish during the negotiations, however, she had not been idle.

" I bought a pair of shoes today," she reported, " lined with flannel to walk about on the bare floors of Italy in the winter."

It was almost her only concession to the tradition of the trousseau.

She was dissatisfied with Henry's conduct of the negotiations for Flush. Greatly daring, she determined to invade Whitechapel herself. Arabel and Henrietta were horrified. She would be robbed, murdered, God knew what, and then what would their father say, they warned her. But Flush's mistress was bold and set off in a cab with only the shivering Wilson to bear her company to the den of thieves. Respectable homes and shops grew dingier and finally made way for the crumbling warrens of the East End. The streets swarmed with ragged, vulgar people, but the two women held on. Ba even ordered a halt at an infamous looking pub to ask the way. A good-natured toper, whom Ba suspected of unnamed and horrible crimes, was eager to be of service. He listened while she explained her mission and then exclaimed:

"Ow, it's Mister Tyler ye want," and he set off at a run to lead the way.

Taylor was not at home, but his wife, " a huge fat bandit," knew what manners should be. She lumbered into the street and, while a curious crowd gathered to stare blankly at so much respectability in a cab, she urged the visitors to come in to wait. Ba declined, left a message that she hoped Mr. Taylor would call about the dog and departed hastily. Without further incident, the adventurers reached the haven of Wimpole Street. A few minutes later Taylor arrived and said that if six guineas were " confided to his honor," Flush would be returned safely and soon. Ba sent down the money, but she was unfortunate in her brothers. Alfred found Taylor in the hall, abused him for a liar, a thief and a swindler and drove the outraged business man into the street, vowing that none of them would ever see the dog again. Ba was so angry she could not even cry. She came downstairs and, although it was getting dark, threatened to drive again to the iniquity of Whitechapel and transact her own affairs. Only by promising the utmost tact, courtesy and abnegation did Septimus persuade her to let him go instead. He performed his mission so ably that at eight

o'clock a woefully thin, dirty, thirsty Flush was back in his mistress's arms.

The marriage could now proceed. No day had yet been fixed, but Robert had borrowed £100 from his father for the necessary expenses until Ba's next quarterly allowance should come due in October. The young man was very independent; he refused to take the money as a wedding gift.

Troubles crowded thick upon them, however. In the excitement of preparation Robert took sick, the first illness of his life, and was in bed for three days. He spent the time assuring Ba that it was nothing. He was right, but she could not believe it until on Tuesday his doctor told him to get up and do as he pleased. He promptly called at No. 50 Wimpole Street, and all Ba's fears were relieved to see how little mark the illness had left upon him.

The very next day her father took it into his head to move at once. He ordered his sons to find a house in which they could live while No. 50 was redecorated. Ba wrote in terror that it would disrupt all their plans. What could they do? Get married at once, Robert answered.

"I will go for a license today and we can be married Saturday," he wrote on Thursday. "I will call tomorrow at 3 and arrange everything with you."

The entire Barrett family, excepting only Ba, had gone on a picnic to Richmond that Friday afternoon when Robert

entered the gloomy old house for the last time. He had the
license in his pocket and together the lovers studied it rapturously. With only Flush around to bother them, they tried
to be calm as they discussed details of the flight. Ba was to
give it out that she was going to call upon the blind Hugh
Boyd. But she meant first to drive to Marylebone Church
where Robert would be waiting with Jim Silverthorne. Jim
could be trusted for one witness to their marriage and Wilson
would be the other.

At last, reluctantly as usual, he took his leave lest the returning picnickers find him in the house. Ba did not want
to see them either and she went early to bed.

Not even her opiate could give her sleep that night. When,
leaning heavily on Wilson's arm, she ventured out into the
street next morning, she staggered so that she could scarcely
stand. Her first visit on her wedding morning was to a
chemist's shop for a bottle of sal volatile. Thus fortified, she
was able to go on, and at 10:45 she marched bravely into
Marylebone Church.

She was pale and twitching, looking many more than her
forty years beside Robert's glowing good looks. Both missed
a good deal of the service. She was filled with dread of the
future. He gloried proudly in the triumph of poetry over
material difficulties and parental objections. He was exalted
far above himself as he slipped the ring, which she had provided, upon her trembling finger. Through it all Ba was

sustained by sentiments that she later tried to put into words, saying:

" In the emotion and confusion there was yet room in me for one thought which was not a feeling — for I thought that of the many, many women who have stood where I stood, and to the same end, not one perhaps, since that building was a church, has had reasons strong as mine for an absolute trust and devotion towards the man she married, — not one! And then I both thought and felt that it was only just for them, those women who were less happy, to have that affectionate sympathy and support and presence of their nearest relations, parent or sister, which failed to *me,* needing it less through being happier! "

In half an hour it was all over and they were saying good-bye at the church door. Sniffing again at the sal volatile, the bride drove off for the promised visit to Boyd while the happy bridegroom paused to note in his pocket-book that this had been their ninety-first meeting.

At one o'clock, while Ba was sitting in Boyd's drawing-room, appalled by the necessity of keeping up a conversation and being served with a glass of wine and a slice of bread and butter in lieu of wedding breakfast and to keep up her strength, Robert was already at home, writing:

" I am all gratitude and all pride. Take every care of *my life* which is in that dearest little hand; try and be composed my beloved.

"Remember to thank Wilson for me."

Browning's more puritanical admirers have constructed a legend that the reason he did not call on his wife during the next week was that his truthful soul revolted at the prospect of asking for "Miss Barrett." He was an honest man, but he did not deserve such a Galahadian reputation. The reason he did not call was that Ba asked him not to. She was afraid that if she saw him she would immediately begin boasting that he was her husband. Meanwhile he did not flinch from addressing letters to "Miss Barrett," and in one of them he said: "Of course, a word brings me as usual to you."

On Saturday, however, Ba was waiting in an agony of impatience for her sisters to come and fetch her away from Boyd's. They appeared at last, and together the three drove, Ba with a cloud before her eyes as she passed Marylebone, back to Wimpole Street. Safe in her own room again, the bride at once seized her pen.

"If either of us two," she wrote, "is to suffer injury and sorrow for what happened there today, I pray that it may fall upon *me!* Nor should I suffer the most pain *that* way. Ask your mother to forgive me, Robert.

"Was I very uncourteous to your cousin? So kind it was in him!"

And then for the first time it occurred to them that the marriage of England's leading poetess to one of the most

promising of the younger poets would be news of the kind that is the life-blood of journalism. Suppose the fact should be discovered prematurely? The newly married couple did not plan to leave just yet but they would have to fly if the news were published to a surprised world.

"Can there be the least danger of the newspapers?" Ba asked apprehensively. "Are those books ever examined by penny-a-liners, do you suppose?"

They were not. The day when the wit and science of mankind would be used by a powerful press to expose the most intimate privacies of the prominent to a gaping public had not yet come. Editors were not more scrupulous; they were only less resourceful, and the marriage register was not a recognized source of news.

Sunday, the day after their marriage, was spent in an enforced idleness that was a great strain on both lovers. They relieved the unhappy tedium to some extent by writing letters to each other, but even they could not write all day. Robert mooned about the house telling anyone who would listen how happy he was, picking up books and throwing them down again, returning to his all-enduring family to sing Ba's praises once more. His mother was ill, but sent loving messages to her new daughter. Sis also sent her regards. That gave Robert an excuse to run up to his room and write another letter to Wimpole Street. In it he assured

Ba that with his own family's love to support them, they would be able to win over hers.

"And your father," he added, "may be sure that while I adore his daughter, it will be impossible for me, under any circumstances, to be wanting in the utmost respect for, and obedience of, himself."

That point off his mind, he wandered downstairs to his own father. Never once had that scholarly gentleman's patience failed. For months he had been gallantly suppressing the inevitable thought that the courtship was a little queer, the marriage rather odd. Whatever opinions he might have had about a wedding which was followed immediately by a separation he kept to himself. He listened to his son's ravings and smiled just as benevolently as he could. He was used to being interrupted. Today he was reading and tried to ignore the boy's uneasy presence. Robert watched him for a moment in silence, but he could not hold his tongue for long.

"Will you not be glad to see your new daughter?" he asked for the twentieth time.

Reluctantly the reader pulled his mind from his book. What, again! But the old smile was on tap and with just as much eager emphasis as he had mustered the first time he answered that question, he replied:

"Indeed I shall."

A long pause, while Robert contemplated the mental

image of his adored and Bob sought for words that would not sound in his own ears so monotonous from uncounted repetition.

"And how I should be glad of her seeing Sis," he managed at last, and picked up his book again with a sigh.

In Wimpole Street the day dragged even more painfully. All morning the Marylebone Church bells rang madly in Ba's ears. She could not relieve her pent up emotions by talking about Robert to anyone and she was not even vouchsafed the alternate boon of solitude. Most of her brothers, both her sisters and a couple of women friends elected that day of all days to entertain poor Ba. Her head nearly split with the noise of so many chattering voices, and when she was alone for a few moments at last, in came Kenyon, demanding as he peered owlishly through his spectacles:

"When did you see Browning?"

"He was here on Friday," she replied, and felt all the effect of the evasion vanishing in the deep blush that colored her pale face while Kenyon smiled sardonically.

It was not until the quiet of evening that she could remember:

"I have a right now openly to love you, and to hear other people call it *a duty* when I do, knowing that if it were a sin it would be done equally. I did hate so to have to take off the ring! You will have to take the trouble of putting it on again some day."

123

Suddenly, to her horror, she discovered that perhaps it was a sin after all, that the marriage was not valid, that the terrible Saturday of nervous fear which, tradition assured her, would make her the happiest woman in the world, had been suffered in vain. Rereading the marriage certificate with gloating eyes she saw that Robert had given "Moulton" as one of her Christian names whereas it was, though seldom used, half of her surname. Robert laughed and insisted it required a greater error than that to upset a legal marriage in the eyes of God and man.

Before they could develop this theme to its proper proportions, George found a house and the Barrett family was given orders to move into it next Monday. The poets were, therefore, forced to fix the previous Saturday for their own departure. More than ever their correspondence became a maze of endearments and practical advice. Voicing the immemorial plea of husbands for as few trunks as possible, Robert suggested cannily:

" Do not trouble yourself with more than is strictly necessary — you can supply all wants at Leghorn or Pisa. Let us be as unencumbered with luggage as possible."

The fewer books, the better, he wrote a day or two later, and conjured Ba to remember that everything was charged for by the ounce. She did even better than he had thought possible, for all her and Wilson's belongings were squeezed

into one light box and a carpetbag. Robert himself required
a portmanteau and a carpetbag. There was only one bit of
excess baggage from Wimpole Street.

"Your letters to me," said Ba, "I take with me, let the
'ounces' cry aloud ever so. I *tried* to leave them and could
not."

Robert took it for granted that she knew her letters to him
would accompany him always. He was more concerned just
then in making sure that the elopement came off according
to plan. That plan was completed by Friday. Her luggage
was smuggled out to him the day before; she and Wilson
would slip from the house on Saturday afternoon; Robert
would be waiting at Hodgeson's, the bookseller around the
corner, from three-thirty to four, and after that let the lions
roar.

On Friday morning he wrote the last letter he was ever to
send her. It was full of information about time-tables, and
for once in his life he showed that by taking pains he could
write quite clearly in short, crisp sentences.

"God bless and strengthen you my ever dearest, dearest,"
he concluded. "I will not trust myself to speak of my
feelings for you. Worship well belongs to such fortitude.
One struggle more. Depend on me. I go to Town about
business.

Your own, own,

R."

Replying that night with an assurance that she would be on time, Ba brought to its end the correspondence that so frankly and proudly revealed the souls of the writers.

" By tomorrow at this time," she thought and put the thought on paper, " I shall have *you* only to love me, my beloved!

" You *only!* As if one said *God only*.

" It is dreadful, dreadful, to have to give pain here by a voluntary act, for the first time in my life.

" Do you pray for me tonight, Robert? Pray for me, and love me, that I may have courage feeling both.

Your own

Ba

" The boxes are *safely sent*. Wilson has been perfect to me. And *I,* calling her ' timid,' and afraid of her timidity! I begin to think none are so bold as the timid, when they are fairly roused."

So to the end the spirit of their courtship was maintained. The ardor of a lover, expressed by poets terrifyingly articulate on paper, the confiding trust in the future, the regrets for their impropriety, their abandonment of everything for each other, and at the very end the tag of philosophy! Even in love they never quite lost the ability to think, and to express their thoughts.

Everyone in the house was packing up in preparation for moving day when Ba walked away from the noisy confusion

of her home to the haven of Robert's love. She did not totter this time, but walked firmly, scorning Wilson's aid. No one seeing her turn the corner would have suspected that here went England's leading poetess on her way to a rendezvous with her poet lover. There were no frills or senseless ribbons on her bonnet. Her dark traveling dress was unadorned save for the locket, containing the lock of Robert's hair, in the hollow of her throat.

At Hodgeson's, Robert idly handled books and watched the door. There she was! He sprang forward, but they did not even touch hands. He managed a respectful bow, she a curtsey and shyly took his arm as they walked sedately from the place without having disturbed by any outward display of affection the musty, hushed solemnity of the bookshop. Their cab waited at the door; their tickets were in Robert's pocket; Wilson was mounting beside the driver. They looked back once towards Wimpole Street. Then he handed Ba royally into the carriage, leaped in beside her and off they drove, leaving literary London with its choicest morsel of gossip since Byron quit the town.

"A little old, too old for Browning," the faithful Arnould reported of her to Dommett, "but then one word covers all, they are in Love who lends his own youth to everything. The old rascal of a father of course tore his beard, foamed at the mouth, and performed all other feats of impotent rage; luckily his wrath is absolutely idle, for she has a small inde-

pendence of some £350 per an., on which they will of course live prosperously."

Perhaps the loyal friend in this gleeful chronicle a little exaggerated Barrett's anger. But at least it was great enough that in the good old style of parental tyrants in an age when " paternal authority " was not a meaningless phrase, he forbad all mention of his daughter's name in his presence, and rejected hotly all advances looking to a reconciliation. Never would he admit the true reason, his outraged vanity, for this unabating rage.

" I had nothing against the young man," he explained, " but my daughter should have been thinking of another world."

Behind the fleeing poets their friends raised a chorus of amazement, and Wordsworth expressed the sentiment of all when he remarked, in a little sharper tone than others would have used:

" So Robert Browning and Elizabeth Barrett have gone off together! Well, I hope they understand each other; no one else can."

TEN

AND POMEGRANATES

THE invaluable Wilson never wrote letters to be treasured by her friends either for friendship's sake or for the use posterity might want to make of them. Neither did she commit her memoirs to paper. The misery of the Brownings' honeymoon, the only unhappy days of their married life, thus lost its only competent chronicler. But Wilson was much too busy to write about her troubles.

A rough crossing of the Channel, accentuating the nervous reaction from so many days of anxiety and daring, left Ba a more than usually helpless invalid. Robert, distracted and dismayed, hovered around her with offers of food and drink. He shared her sleeplessness, was tireless in the search for rugs, cushions, cups of tea, sheltered retreats on deck. But in spite, perhaps because of his every effort, they were all three exhausted when they rattled into Paris to beseech the good offices of an amazed friend, Anna Jameson, who had known Ba and Robert quite well separately but had never been aware of their acquaintance, much less their marriage. Three weeks earlier Mrs. Jameson, then preparing for her own trip

to the Continent, had called on Ba at Wimpole Street to urge the poetess to go along. Ba had protested that she was too ill for such an undertaking.

"I am forced to be satisfied with sofa and silence," she had lied.

Now in Paris she really was ill, and Robert was too much disturbed for their friend to bother them with questions. Her competent care quickly restored them to strength and confidence and sustained them mightily as they proceeded with her by easy stages to Pisa. The strange sights, the delightfully warm sunshine, the lazy, comfortable progress of three weeks broken by many stops at inviting villages along the pleasant countryside revived Ba's energy and Robert's cheerfulness. Laughter and eager conversation filled their carriage, and when they reached Pisa at last only the good Mrs. Jameson was tired. Her friends were fresh for their new life.

Duly settled in comfortable lodgings, they were so little worried about the future that their traveling companion, leaving them to themselves with no little relief, was moved to express to other friends some gloomy forebodings about the troubles so sure to descend upon poets thus carelessly tempting fate with the naive improvidence of their kind.

"Both excellent," she wrote, "but God help them, for I know not how the two poet heads and poet hearts will get on in this prosaic world."

She need not have worried. The apparent carelessness was born of a sense of complete security. With Wilson to care for them and Flush for company, they lived on dreams and "thrushes and chianti with a miraculous cheapness." In England the Barrett household might be swept by violent storms, Wordsworth elaborate his bitter jests, the press exclaim in sympathy or amazement or ridicule, their friends recover as best they could from their surprise. But in Pisa Ba was writing:

"Even the pouring of the coffee is a divided labor and the ordering of the dinner is quite out of my hands. As for me, when I am so good as to let myself be carried upstairs, and so angelical as to sit still on the sofa and so considerate, moreover, as *not* to put my foot into a puddle, why *my* duty is considered done to a perfection which is worthy of all adoration."

Petted, guarded and nursed with a devotion she had never imagined before, Ba suddenly found herself able to walk upstairs alone, to move about the streets and live in general after the fashion of a normal person. Robert's mania for carrying her about in his arms was soon due more to his pride in his strength and a masculine desire for using it on behalf of frail femininity than to any real necessity. Meanwhile she owed her cure to his lack of a real, comprehending concern for her health. Robert did not understand illness, and the physicians of the age would have been horrified at his treatment of a consumptive. He actually kept her out of doors. He ordered excursions into the country because he believed happiness was better than repose, and he knew Ba would find happiness in the sights he could show her. He was right. Soon she was being dragged up mountains, riding donkeys over the hillsides, taking long walks, standing in galleries for hours to be instructed in and argue about Italian art. This last was a field in which Robert was already so expert that Rossetti considered his knowledge beyond that of anyone else on earth and Ruskin mourned that he had needed thirty pages to tell what Browning could put into thirty lines.

It was characteristic of Robert that he was far prouder of his wife's health than of his own learning. Indeed, he was childishly enthusiastic about her strength; he bragged about it to anyone who would listen.

" I have to tell him," Ba wrote, " that he really must not go telling everybody how his wife walked here with him or walked there with him, as if a wife with two feet were a miracle in nature."

She was the only one in the household who remained well. Flush was the first patient, for he was almost at once beset by a particularly virulent variety of Italian flea and Ba sent off a rush order to England for remedies. Robert fell a victim to a slight fever and for several days his wife suffered agonies of fear, but the illness was short. Wilson contracted a worse

fever, but that was not nearly so terrifying. Wilson could, they found, be spared if necessary.

" I have acquired a heap of practical philosophy," Ba reported after being deprived for a week of her maid's services, " and have learnt how it is possible (in certain conditions of the human frame) to comb out and twist up one's own hair, and lace one's very own stays and cause hooks and eyes to meet behind one's very own back."

Robert was just as inordinately proud of his wife's genius as he was of her health, while she concentrated her enthusiasms on his poems. He was never tired of telling how Ba could work under any conditions, even with people chattering in the same room. Most of her writing was done on the arm of her chair in odd moments. He marvelled that she could calmly accept any intrusion, however trivial, stop in the middle of a line, thrust the paper away and return later to take up the thread of her thought as easily as if it had never been interrupted. He himself, although his hours of toil were most irregular, demanded peace and quiet. While they were still at Pisa he was revising his poems for an edition of his collected works.

" They are to be so clear that everyone who has understood them hitherto will lose all distinction," Ba boasted, with rather premature optimism, but her husband was becoming sensitive to the ever recurring charge of intentional obscurity.

She was not yet exhibiting her writings, and even when Robert entered the room she concealed the manuscript inside a book or under her cushions. Nor did he have anything new to show her. For nearly three years he did no original writing at all, content to revise his old work, explaining that he was " paying peculiar attention to the objections made against certain obscurities." For the rest he was much too busy teaching Ba to be happy, which was more immediately remunerative than anything he ever wrote, to bother about the great poems for which his friends were waiting.

Ba grew more critical of other men's works as she saw more of the world, and without losing her admiration for Tennyson, she was now able to recognize some of his weaknesses. Once she had actually considered him Browning's superior, but she had the grace to be ashamed of that. One of the women in his new poem, she now complained, was only a rose.

" And ' a rose,' one might beg all poets to observe, is as precisely *sensual* as fricasseed chicken, or even boiled beef and carrots."

Nevertheless when gossip concerning the future Laureate's romances in real life reached them, Ba wrote indignantly:

" I must either pity or despise a woman who could have married Tennyson and chose a common man. If happy in her choice I despise her. I personally would rather be teased a little and smoked over a good deal by a man whom I could

look up to and be proud of than have my feet kissed all day by a Mr. Smith in boots and a waistcoat and thereby chiefly distinguished."

Her own happiness plainly accounted for whatever might seem a trifle extravagant in her views on marriage. For Robert combined, she found, the virtues of genius and the more ordinary qualities of a Mr. Smith without any of the drawbacks of either. He did not tease her nor smoke nor kiss her feet all day. But he showed her his poems, asked her advice, disputed with a wealth of quotation on moot points of literature and history, planned future trips, ordered dinner, wore his coat in her presence, found lodgings, made friends she liked and — best of all — acted always with the devotion of a lover and the camaraderie of a friend who recognizes that the loved one is also a human being.

The promise of his letters to her was being fulfilled. Actually Robert asked nothing except to be with Ba and write, and he did not do much writing. Even years after their marriage he refused to go to dinner-parties which would have been too strenuous for her. In those first few years he never went out at all without her and since she did not leave home in the evenings, Robert, the great diner out, the dancer, the convivial soul of a thousand parties, remained happily by his own fireside, roasting chestnuts, reading, talking or playing the piano. He had always known what he wanted, so he was not surprised to find that this new mode of life was much more fun than the gayest of London seasons.

Complete solitude they neither sought nor desired. After a soul-satisfying stay in Pisa, they drifted into Florence and for the next fifteen years their lives centered about this most charming of Italian cities. Wandering about the country, carelessly footloose as long as the weather remained warm enough for Ba, they were always finding good, intelligent, talkative folk, sometimes English but more often American, with whom to eat strawberries and cream and drink a glass of wine. Painters, sculptors, writers, serious men and casual dilettantes discovered that conversation was always to be had at the Brownings. Robert could be counted upon to hold forth, learned, eloquent and anecdotal, while Ba quietly applied the corrective of humor and a certain incorrigible sanity of outlook.

Physically she grew stronger at Florence than she had been at Pisa, and Robert's boasting increased proportionately. Together they scrambled about the mountains, Robert on foot or horseback and Ba aboard a donkey or dragged exhaustingly aloft in a basket. She even made her way up three thousand feet of olive clad slopes to Vallombrosa where together they gazed in awe upon the green hills, looked down upon beloved Florence snuggling cozily in the arms of the Arno and explored the forests around the old

monastery which was the only habitation on the heights. It was too good to last. The austere meditations of the monks of Vallombrosa were disturbed by the presence of two women. After five days Robert was informed that he might stay, but Ba and Wilson would have to go. They had come for two months, but now they wound their way down the mountain to Florence, crying out against the injustice of fate and the scruples of celibates.

However, Florence proved ample compensation for all they had missed or ever could miss. In the beauty of the old city, surrounded by congenially appreciative souls, treated to the indolent, good-natured politeness of Tuscany, the Brownings developed an intense Italian nationalism that colored all their poetry and molded their lives.

It was not a new development for Robert. Ever since he had listened in the library at Camberwell to his father's stories of emperors, grand dukes, artists and priests, he had felt a kinship with the country of his dreams. Now that his dreams had come true, the feeling was stronger than ever. His earliest poems had dealt with Italy and after his visits to the peninsula he had expressed in his verse the aspirations of Italian patriotism. His

> "I would grasp Metternich until
> I felt his wet red throat distil
> In blood thro' these two hands"

137

was a more virile cry of hate than the Italy of 1845, crushed under long generations of unremitting oppression, could have uttered for herself.

All the poet in the man, all the zest for living that made the poet, had found an outlet in his ardent devotion to Italy, the Italy which was still only a name that idealists whispered reverently, hopefully or wistfully in their murmurings of the future goal of all endeavor. His emotional response to this land was very different from the sturdy, critical British affection which he continued to hold for his native island. It was Browning the man of fashion, the playwright, the respectable citizen who embodied the virtues of the typical Englishman. It was Browning the poet, the worshipper of beauty, the genius in the art of living who cherished a love of Italy.

Ba's passion for the country was to become even less restrained, more compelling as she grew ever more grateful for the happiness she found there. But in these first months she saw beside the splendors of the Italian scene only a decadent art, lethargy, meanness and decay.

"It is well that they have great memories," she wrote. "Nothing else lives."

She could not see beneath the pettiness of Italian politics the current that was sweeping Europe on to '48. Austria had never seemed more secure in her authority. Metternich's policy of Germanizing the people was opposed only by

the efforts of a few such despised exiles as Mazzini. Cavour was not yet even a name to his countrymen. Victor Emmanuel was only the Crown Prince of insignificant Piedmont. Garibaldi was fighting the battles of freedom across the Atlantic. Yet there were signs of the coming storm; there always are for those who come after the event. Pope Gregory XVI had just died, detested and despised, and optimists were seeing in his successor, the comparatively young, kindly, well-intentioned Pio Nono, the herald of a new era of liberty.

"A liberal Pope is inconceivable," the astute Metternich had said, and had made that a corner-stone of his policy.

Pius seemed about to disprove the theory. When he ascended the Throne of Saint Peter in 1846, he gave every appearance of liberalism. He inaugurated his reign with a general amnesty in the Papal States, authorized the publication of newspapers that actually discussed politics — hitherto such were banned in Rome — consented to the innovation of granting State offices to laymen, and even discussed the possibility of building a railway through his domains. The party of dreamers whose ideal was a confederation of Italian states under the Pope's presidency hailed His Holiness as the prophet of Italian freedom. But although the first faint stirrings of the uprising that was to come were evident in the response to the new measures, Metternich was not alarmed. He knew Pius to be an autocrat by temperament, desirous

of giving happiness to his subjects but hotly resenting any effort on their part to take it for themselves.

Robert shared the general admiration for the new Pope's apparent liberalism, a sentiment which had even reached England, whose Government was now considering the appointment of a Minister to Rome. Robert's old partiality for diplomacy, strengthened by his very real desire to strike a blow for Italian freedom prompted him to offer his services as secretary to the Legation. In a letter to Monckton Milnes he promised to work like a horse for the success of the mission. But after much talk and political bickering, there was no mission and Robert had to content himself with merely watching the revolution get under way. It received no more assistance from him than a few poetic cheers, but when the Pope's real nature was made manifest to the world, the poet was glad that he had not been given an opportunity to display his diplomatic talents on behalf of such a man.

Ba did not even see the shadows of the coming events. The apathy of the people, the resigned cheerfulness with which they bore their poverty, the absence of such an assertive band of artists and scholars as almost deafened London, the indifference to politics, the circulating libraries that did not lend books, the "refined and cultured Italian society" that never read books, the existence of modern literature only in translations — these were her first impressions of Italy.

However, the Brownings were not too much concerned with politics themselves just yet. Robert spent long hours teaching Ba to appreciate the works of the Italian masters. As they tramped through gallery, palace and church, he gave his entranced bride long, expert lectures on the superiority over all others of the colorful Italian school. They watched the peasants toiling languidly among their vines and reached the conclusion, a startling one for idealists of the 'forties, that perhaps it might take more than a theoretical political liberty to wash those faces clean, put nourishing food into those bent bodies and brains into those unthinking heads. This they saw in their quiet journeys from city to city, but the knowledge was soon swept away by the excitement of revolution.

In Rome they saw the splendid pageantry of the Papacy in the last days of its temporal power, admired the beauty of it while their Puritan instincts revolted at an ignorant mob's pious adoration of gaudy symbols. They stood in the midst of the filthy, noisome crowds whose presence insulted the architectural masterpieces in which they congregated. They listened, with a rapture that actually enabled them to ignore the smells, to the majesty of church music flawlessly performed while His Holiness with the traditional proud humility washed the feet of "the rummest set of customers I ever saw." The Brownings were quite ecstatic, and a little superior, about it all.

Within a year they knew Italy would remain their home forever. That knowledge had come to them when they first came into Florence, the city of delightful indolence, content to bask in its own charms. There were a great many English in the place, the Brownings had not made a new discovery, but they decided to tolerate their countrymen, reflecting complacently that they needed to know only the interesting members of the colony.

They found lodgings in an apartment of the mansion that had been the ancestral home of the Counts Guidi. On the Via Maggiore, a street wider than most, it faced San Felice Church and was directly across from the Pitti Palace, then the residence of the Grand Duke. The Brownings were attracted by the fine simplicity of the architecture without, and the blaze of life-giving sunshine within. The place was admirably proportioned, beautifully located, exactly adapted to their needs, well within their means and on Ba's bedroom floor were emblazoned the arms of the last Count Guidi.

Robert's pre-marital fears of financial difficulties had been quite groundless. They saved money, for when Robert was married he determined that he would never again publish anything " at the author's risk," and Ba had long ago abandoned that luxury.

" We scarcely spend three hundred," she wrote, setting at rest Mrs. Jameson's anxieties concerning impractical poets, "and I have every luxury I ever had; and Robert

wouldn't sleep, I think, if an unpaid bill dragged itself by any chance into another week."

There was no necessity for unpaid bills. In addition to Ba's £350, they had £100 a year which Kenyon insisted they take from him; he felt it was the least he could do for such magnificently mad lovers who owed the inception of their romance to his friendly chatter. Neither Ba nor Robert had any false pride about taking such a subsidy from a patron who asked no return. But their income did not stop there either. Actually their books, given impetus by the publicity attending their marriage, began to sell in royalty producing quantities. They got enough from this source in 1847 and 1848 to pay for the furnishings of their apartment in Casa Guidi. Of course they were in luck that the antique furniture and hangings that they loved were rendered marvellously cheap by the revolutions. But they were well satisfied with the revenue from their work.

It was the more remarkable because Ba, whose poetry sold best, sent nothing new to the printer but devoted almost all her attention to the secret manuscript which must have caused Robert many moments of silent wonderment. But he kept his curiosity well hidden. He had far too much respect for his wife's privacy ever to question anything she might be doing.

ELEVEN

REVOLUTION

THE first anniversary of the Brownings' marriage was a great day in Florence. All the city was in a state of wild rejoicing, bursting with a patriotic fervor that was a fit prologue to the year of revolutions. As Ba and Robert recalled to each other the terrors and joys of the morning in Marylebone Church just a year ago, the Grand Duke Leopold II of Tuscany was announcing to his people that it graciously pleased him to grant them a Civic Guard.

He did it with just the same large careless gesture, the same condescending, pitying smile, the same weak generosity as he would have displayed in tossing a coin to an importunate beggar. He wanted to be rid of a petty annoyance, and he did not mind achieving popularity cheaply. To his people the edict seemed a bold stroke for liberty. Austria had threatened to occupy any Italian State whose ruler dared to make such concessions to popular demand. But while Tuscany applauded the heroism of its sovereign, the Duke was already deadening his fear with the thought that Austria was very far away and that a concession granted in one decree

could be withdrawn by another before his Imperial cousin in Vienna had time to be really unpleasant about such a show of independence.

All this day of September twelfth the happy Florentines had filled the narrow streets congratulating each other on the possession of so noble a lord, crying his praises, assuring themselves that a new freedom was about to descend upon humble folk now that there was a Civic Guard to defend their homes. Thus easily were men's aspirations appeased in 1847.

In honor of the Civic Guard, the stone walls of Florence were bright with flags and banners while forty thousand cheering, singing, grateful and optimistic enthusiasts marched down upon the Grand Ducal Palace just across from Casa Guidi to express their vociferous thanks for what they were sure could be nothing less than the dawn of the millenium. The millenium is always just about to dawn in the happy days when revolutions are young and promising.

Arm in arm Ba and Robert stood at their window, waving and shouting with the best of patriots until Ba's wrist ached from so much flaunting of her handkerchief. They were being treated to the sort of spectacle Robert loved most. Here were human beings giving lusty vent to their emotions against a background of brilliant flags and historic buildings. The frenzied yelling, the surging disorderly ranks of the marchers, the rude banners with their inscriptions " Union

of Italy," " Liberty," " Viva Pio Nono," " Viva Leopoldo,"
the sight of the Grand Duke weeping for joy in the midst
of his family at this display of affection from his loyal people,
the men kissing each other in the excitement, the women
tossing their babies in the air, the very children screaming
shrilly as if they knew what it was all about — the whole
panorama of a city gone mad with joy sent the blood tingling
through his body, gave him the keen sense of being alive
in a good world. Only moments like this assuaged his
nervous energy. But it was Ba who found the scene worthy
of their art and in " Casa Guidi Windows " was to give her
version of the new era.

A few months later she and Robert felt themselves indeed
a part of the revolution as, on a crisp evening in February,
they watched Leopold carried home from the Opera on the
shoulders of an adoring mob. During the day the Duke had
paid his reverence to the shibboleths of the time by promul-
gating a Constitution for Tuscany. The two poets stood on
their balcony, clapping, as the spirit of liberalism stormed
past in the dark night, " a great flock of stars sweeping up
the piazza but not in silence."

From that day on Ba and Robert were enrolled among
the most ardent of Italian patriots. Their admiration for
Leopold increased, and his popularity continued. As the
revolutionary spirit swept northward from Sicily, where
the first uprising of '48 had occurred in January, they spoke

146

scornfully of their compatriots. The English were flying in scores from Florence as the white-coated Austrians maneuvered leisurely across Tuscany towards the capital, and Leopold was reminded that he had a cousin. The Brownings professed to be much more afraid of the mosquitoes than of the Austrian troops, and Ba, seeing the city emptied of its English colony as fast as the stages could accommodate the refugees, sneered:

"Always first fly the majors and gallant captains, unless there's a general."

For themselves they welcomed the crisis which enabled them to buy Casa Guidi cheaply and furnish the rooms nobly at small expense. Real estate was falling fast in the face of the advancing Austrians and the timid were glad to get any price for belongings which might be the object of loot before a purchaser could enjoy them. The Brownings would never have been able to furnish a home nearly so well save for the fabulous cheapness of everything in these days of uncertainty. Robert had a morbid horror of going into debt, and Ba could not reason him out of it. Although she and the dealers in Florence assured him that his credit as an Englishman was good, he insisted on paying at once for what he took.

Not even the satisfaction they derived from gazing upon their new splendor could compensate for the pain they suffered as they watched disaster spreading over the land. They

had entered into the cry for a free Italy with such utter abandon that, more than most Italians, they were saddened by the obviously approaching collapse of the liberal movement. With despair they realized that Italians might cheer more easily for liberty than Englishmen, but they would not work and fight for it so hard. Revolutions were not permitted to interfere with the pleasures of the people, and adversity failed to arouse that dogged persistence upon which Englishmen prided themselves. These Italians were content to wait for another day.

Ba and Robert walked about as usual to see the palaces and galleries, to visit friends, to watch the sunsets on the Arno. They made an excursion to Fano, which was too hot for any use. Ba spent all her time lying on the sofa as thinly clad as decency would permit, even more thinly clad, Robert thought, but he crushed his scruples for her comfort and murmured reassuringly, "Never mind, dear." But Ba was wearing only a wrapper over her petticoat and felt strangely immodest whenever the waiter came in with their meals. The strain was too much, and they returned to Florence.

The Tuscans had by this time shouted themselves out. After all the Grand Duke's gestures and tears, after all the processions and flag waving, after all the spontaneous carnivals that sent floods of paraders roaring down the streets, Tuscany lay quite still under the Austrian threats, " eating

ices," as Ba complained, "and keeping the feast of the Madonna." She had learned without losing her affection for them or her ardor for their liberation from the Austrian rule that Italians "have only the rhetoric of patriots and soldiers." She and Robert were impatient. They grew quite scornful as they saw conspirators display a great deal more anxiety about playing their parts well than about the success of their plot. As Englishmen, they were disgusted with the childishness of calling off a revolution because of rain. They did not understand that the would-be rebels could not go through with their plans with the verve demanded by tradition if the banners got wet, the soldiers of liberty chilled, the parade to celebrate victory drowned in a dull drizzle.

At last, however, the weather was propitious and Leghorn rose against and deposed the Grand Duke. Seven weeks later a peasant counter-revolution restored Leopold to his throne. Ba always insisted the counter-revolution succeeded only because the Leghornese patriots would not pay for their drinks at the cafes. A succession of benevolently despotic rulers had spoiled the Tuscans for serious rebellion. Leopold's early and hasty concessions had swept his mercurial subjects on to renewed demands, it is true, and a year after he gave them a Constitution the Republic was proclaimed while the Leghornese swilled unpaid-for wine and bragged about their prowess in war. However, the peasants preferred Leopold to the Leghorn bombasts. They invited their Grand

Duke home again. He was by this time so thoroughly frightened by his experiments in liberalism that he brought with him an Austrian army that remained for six years and cost him all his popularity.

As '48 wore onward in an ever accelerating collapse of constitutions and republics, two blessings consoled the Brownings for the ruin of their ideals. The hated Metternich had passed from power forever and Ba was carrying a child. Consequently they were very happy, despite the swift debacle in Europe. They observed the gory course of the Commune in Paris with interest and from a distance, the rise of the Second Republic and the election of Prince Louis Napoleon as President. Germany with its constitutions and revolutions was only attractive because of the embarrassment provided for Austria, but they spent long hours debating the German Question. For it was with discussion of politics that they disguised the fears that intruded on their domestic happiness. The tragedy of Italy and free political institutions was something of a relief from the contemplation of the more poignant dangers that were so easily imagined by a pregnant woman of forty-two who for most of twenty years had been too sick to walk.

Robert Wiedemann Barrett Browning was born on March 9, 1849, just two weeks before Radetzky smothered the last flame of revolt at Novaro and brought Victor Emmanuel to the throne of Piedmont while his father, Charles Albert,

retired to a monastery to die. In Tuscany the collapse had come even sooner. A few weeks before her confinement, Ba had seen a tree of liberty planted near Casa Guidi to the accompaniment of wild cries of "Viva la Republica!" as the men of Leghorn swept into the city and the Grand Duke fled towards Austrian headquarters. Three days after her child was born the same men were yelling "Viva Leopoldo!" as they hastily uprooted the tree and waited for the white uniformed troops of the oppressor to escort the Grand Duke back to the palace.

Lying near the window, she heard the sudden rattle of shots as a few Florentines made a last stand in the streets for Tuscan independence. Very frightened she was, for Robert had gone out for a walk. He, too, listened to the quick volleys of the troops and the scattered shots of the patriots while he strolled calmly along the Arno waiting for the battle to get out of his way and permit him to get safely home again. The fighting died out and he returned with the story of his adventure to find that Dr. Harding, Ba's physician, had been before him with an even more exciting tale. Coming to visit his patient, he had without warning walked into the very midst of the shooting and had taken hasty refuge in a stable. After the troops had driven the revolutionaries back to their cellars and their plots, the trembling doctor found that his hiding place had become a prison. He cried long for aid, and when it finally came he found that the bar to his resumption

of professional calls had been four corpses piled up where they had fallen against the stable door.

The revolution in Tuscany was over and others in Europe were dying too. While Robert with his wisdom in the matter of training animals cured Flush of his jealousy of the baby and taught the dog to guard the cradle, he spared a sigh for Sicily where King " Bomba " was bloodily stamping out the revolt, and for his friends in Rome who were seeing the short-lived Roman Republic annihilated in a lethargic siege by soldiers of the new French Republic. As Garibaldi's Legion wound through the hills on the beginning of its dolorous march to the sea, French bayonets escorted back to Rome a Pope whom exile and bitterness had cured forever of any leanings towards liberalism or reform. Mazzini's vision of what he believed to be the inevitable history of the Eternal City, that the Rome of the Caesars having become the Rome of the Popes must now become the Rome of the people, vanished in the night with Garibaldi's picturesque caped figure.

> " So with a sullen ' All's for best,'
>   The land seems settling to its rest,"

Robert had written, and he now thought the words had been prophetic. But Italy retained the habits formed in '48 and these, repressed but unbroken, only awaited more auspicious days.

WALTER SAVAGE LANDOR

" All in a curl and white bubblement of beauty."

Robert was forming some new habits of his own. He was surprised, although no one else was, to find in himself the makings of a fond father. He was also an excellent nurse-maid, much better than Ba, who all her life remained exceedingly awkward with her hands. Robert never missed the baby's bath, and he enjoyed walking the armful of son up and down the terrace, laughing gleefully as the tiny fists clutched at his whiskers. They could both amuse themselves in that way by the hour.

The death of his mother a few days after his son was born was the first real sorrow Robert had ever known. Until he met Ba, his mother had been the chief love of his youth, and he was one of those beings who need love for happiness. Her silent kindliness, such a contrast to his own demonstrative nature, had made it easy for him to idealize her and now, although he had Ba, he brooded miserably for days.

" He has loved his mother as such passionate natures only can love," wrote the sympathetic wife, " and I never saw a man so bowed down in an extremity of sorrow — never."

The smoothness of his life had not fitted him to withstand tragedy, and he felt too much the joy of existence to console himself with the thought that death spared his mother much suffering. But the same superlatively healthy emotions which produced his sorrow brought him back to the pleasures of the present.

Ba regained her strength with amazing rapidity and the

family spent the summer at the Baths of Lucca. Metternich
had referred to Lucca as the most charming spot in the
world, but fortunately the Brownings did not know that.
They could never have enjoyed a place where the tyrant had
been amused. As it was, they had a glorious summer, climbing the hills, writing, weighing the baby, who, according to
their unprejudiced judgment, was the finest specimen of humanity ever seen in an unappreciative world. However, the
weight was not much, and because he remained so small they
began to call him " Penini " after Michael Angelo's gigantic
figure of the Appenino.

During their stay at Lucca, Robert set to work at last, and
quite regularly for him, on some new poems. The eminently
satisfactory sales of '47 and '48 had ceased. " Paracelsus " and
the " Bells and Pomegranates " had glutted their very limited
market and for months now he had not received a penny
from his publishers. But they were ready to accept anything
he would do for them, and at their own risk. So nearly
every morning just after breakfast he spent several hours on
his " Men and Women," the series into which he poured all
the gifts of his genius. Men of all ages, all conditions, all
creeds, all degrees of virtue spoke through him, not always
as clearly as one might have wished, but always with beauty
and vigor. A firm believer in conventional Christianity,
he could yet appreciate the pagan sceptic Cleon's fear of
death and voice for him, in reply to a suggestion that an

artist is immortal while kings are merely clay, the ter-
rible cry:

> " Thou diest while I survive?
> Say rather that my fate is deadlier still,
> In this, that every day my sense of joy
> Grows more acute, my soul (intensified
> By power and insight) more enlarged, more keen;
> While every day my hairs fall more and more,
> My hand shakes, and the heavy years increase —
> The horror quickening still from year to year,
> The consummation coming past escape
> When I shall know most, and yet least enjoy —
> When all my works wherein I prove my worth,
> Being present still to mock me in men's mouths,
> Alive still, in the praise of such as thou,
> I, I the feeling, thinking, acting man,
> The man who loved his life so over-much,
> Sleep in my urn."

With complete understanding of the men of antiquity, he
could allow the Arab physician, fresh from an interview with
the revivified Lazarus, to say:

> " Thou wilt object — Why have I not ere this
>   Sought out the sage himself, the Nazarene
>   Who wrought this cure, inquiring at the source,

Conferring with the frankness that befits?
Alas! it grieveth me, the learned leech
Perished in a tumult many years ago,
Accused, — our learning's fate, — of wizardry."

The most hopeful of men, he could, for as long as it took
him to write the lines, share Andrea del Sarto's hopeless disillusion of disappointed genius:

" I do what many dream of, all their lives,
  — Dream? strive to do, and agonize to do,
  And fail in doing. I could count twenty such
  On twice your fingers, and not leave this town,
  Who strive — you don't know how the others strive
  To paint a little thing like that you smeared
  Carelessly passing with your robes afloat, —
  Yet do much less, so much less, Someone says,
  (I know his name, no matter) — so much less!
  Well, less is more, Lucrezia: I am judged.
  There burns a truer light of God in them,
  In their vexed beating stuffed and stopped-up brain,
  Heart, or whate'er else, than goes on to prompt
  This low-pulsed forthright craftsman's hand of mine.
  Their works drop groundward, but themselves, I know,
  Reach many a time a heaven that's shut to me,
  Enter and take their place there sure enough,

Though they come back and cannot tell the world.
My works are nearer heaven, but I sit here."

But mixed in with the men of complex minds and mixed
motives were quite simple heroes, and beside the most subtle of his characters Browning placed the figure of "The
Patriot":

"It was roses, roses, all the way,
    With myrtle mixed in my path like mad:
The house-roofs seemed to heave and sway,
    The church-spires flamed, such flags they had,
A year ago on this very day.

The air broke into a mist with bells,
    The old walls rocked with the crowd and cries.
Had I said, "Good folk, mere noise repels —
    But give me your sun from yonder skies!"
They had answered, "And afterward, what else?"

Alack, it was I who leaped at the sun
    To give it my loving friends to keep!
Naught man could do, have I left undone:
    And you see my harvest, what I reap
This very day, now a year is run.

There's nobody on the house-tops now —
    Just a palsied few at the windows set;

For the best of the sight is, all allow,
 At the Shambles' Gate — or, better yet,
By the very scaffold's foot, I trow.

I go in the rain, and, more than needs,
 A rope cuts both my wrists behind;
And I think, by the feel, my forehead bleeds,
 For they fling, whoever has a mind,
Stones at me for my year's misdeeds.

Thus I entered, and thus I go!
 In triumphs, people have dropped down dead.
"Paid by the world, what dost thou owe
 Me?" — God might question; now instead,
'Tis God shall repay: I am safer so."

One morning as he stood gazing out of the window, thinking of his "Men and Women" and waiting for the breakfast things to be cleared away so that he might use the table, he heard a rustling behind him. Ba's hand was on his shoulder and she thrust something bulky into his pocket. Before he could turn she had fled from the room. Puzzled and wondering what all this mystery could mean, he drew from the pocket a sheaf of papers covered with his wife's neat writing. An hour later he was still standing by the window, but his cheeks were wet with tears. He had finished reading "Sonnets from the Portuguese," the product of Ba's many secret sessions with pen and ink, the verses which she had

promised years ago that he might see " some day." Page after page he read, and even his exalted conception of her gifts for love and for poetry was raised still higher as the Sonnets poured out for him the crescendo of passion that reached its climax with:

" How do I love thee? Let me count the ways.
  I love thee to the depth and breadth and height
  My soul can reach, when feeling out of sight
  For the ends of being and ideal grace.
  I love thee to the level of every day's
  Most quiet need, by sun and candlelight.
  I love thee freely, as men strive for right.
  I love thee purely, as they turn from praise.
  I love thee with the passion put to use
  In my old griefs, and with my childhood's faith.
  I love thee with a love I seemed to lose
  With my lost saints. I love thee with the breath,
  Smiles, tears, of all my life; and, if God choose,
  I shall but love thee better after death."

Robert finished the manuscript so torn by emotion that he was quite weak. He rushed to Ba to tell her all he felt, but when he found her he could not say a word. Nor could she. Once more they were as they had been in the gloomy old room in Wimpole Street, inarticulate but rapturous in their love.

As yet the poems bore no title, that under which they were published being suggested later by Robert. When she wrote them Ba had no thought of publication; they were her gift to Robert, not to the world.

"But I dared not," he explained many years afterwards, "reserve to myself the finest sonnets written in any language since Shakespeare's."

TWELVE

IN BOHEMIA

I T was five years before Robert published his answer. Meanwhile he lived up to a standard of perfection that amazed Fanny Kemble, who spent some of her vacations from the stage in Italy near the Brownings. The actress was a frequent visitor at Casa Guidi where she talked shop with Robert, who never ceased to be drawn towards the theater. She also admired greatly the atmosphere of domestic bliss that pervaded the house so perpetually that some guests thought it a little too impeccable to be real. But not the accomplished Fanny.

" He is," she said of her host, " the only man I ever knew who behaved like a Christian to his wife."

After the first few years of marriage, he and Ba had both become articulate enough with either tongue or pen to give expression to their love on the slightest provocation. Both of them were sentimental romanticists, never tired of speaking endearments or listening to them. Not even their pride in the boy Penini's health, good looks, charm and intelligence (they attributed to their son all these qualities in unbounded measure) could interrupt their incorrigible love-making.

As if this were not happiness enough, they had the delights of friendship and travel. From Florence to Siena to Rome to Lucca and back to Florence again they wandered ceaselessly with only very occasional visits to London and Paris to rouse them from the indolence of Italy. Everywhere they went they were the center for a group of friends to whom they could listen with delight and talk with abandon.

" He is slight," William Wetmore Story wrote of Robert, " with straight black hair, small eyes wide apart which he twitches constantly together, a smooth face, a slightly aquiline nose and manners nervous and rapid. He has great vivacity, but not the least humor, some sarcasm, considerable critical faculty, and very great frankness and friendliness of manner and mind. Mrs. Browning used to sit buried up in a large easy chair, listening and talking very quietly and pleasantly with nothing of that peculiarity which one would expect from reading her poems. Her eyes are small, her mouth large, she wears a cap and long curls. Very unaffected and pleasant and simple-hearted."

Robert's smoothness of face was a temporary affair and one of his minor tragedies. Ba, who admired hirsute adornments with a quite incomprehensible fervor, wrote:

" He was in a state of bilious irritability on the morning of his arrival in Rome from exposure to the sun or some

such cause, and in a fit of suicidal impatience shaved away his whole beard, whiskers and all! I *cried* when I saw him, I was so horror-struck I might have gone into hysterics and still been reasonable, for no human being was ever so disfigured by so simple an act. Of course I said when I recovered breath and voice that everything was at an end between him and me if he didn't let it all grow again directly and (upon the further advice of his looking glass) he yielded the point and the beard grew. But it grew *white* which was the just punishment of the gods — our sins leave traces."

Their friends did not take it quite so hard, and in spite of the poet's disfigurement they continued to come to the house. Story, laboring heroically under the handicap of being the son of his father, the late Chief Justice of the United States Supreme Court, was the closest companion in the Brownings' Italian idyll. Turned from the law to art by the commission of his fellow Bostonians to write a biography and carve a statue of his famous father, the man from Massachusetts had become a confirmed exile. His sculpture was much admired in its day and his writing, too, found a few to give it praise, for he was something of a critic of all the arts and a kindly critic at that. He himself found his greatest happiness in his friendships. His children were Pen Browning's constant playmates, and the parents were almost as often together. Robert, Story thought, had only one real flaw; he

did not smoke. Apparently the sculptor did not mind absence of humor.

When the wine was poured at Casa Guidi or at the Story home, the glasses were in the hands of men and women who devoted themselves with leisurely intensity to the art of living well and with a manner. Frederick Tennyson, the poet's brother, would leave off holding concerts with his forty fiddlers in the big, bare hall of his palace to pass the time of day with the Brownings. Isa Blagden, the shy daughter of a Hindu princess and an English colonial, would be there to adore Robert unobtrusively, help Ba serve refreshments and exercise her gift for encouraging literary folk to talk freely. Not that they needed much encouragement.

Mrs. Jameson was a frequent visitor, for she was often in Florence to write, rather badly but with some success, about Italian art. She never ceased to marvel at the success of the marriage which she had seen start out so unfortunately in Paris. The Hawthornes were almost as familiar as the Storys, and it was remarked that Nathaniel did not talk as much as his compatriot. Ba rather mothered the younger Lytton, who was just of age and such a good, intelligent youth. She and Robert liked him greatly, but they were sure the future Ambassador and Viceroy did not have the qualities necessary to success in diplomacy, in which the young man was starting a career as attaché to the British Legation in Tuscany.

Harriet Beecher Stowe came, talked at great length about

truth and faith, and impressed Ba much more by her belief in spiritualism than by her " Uncle Tom's Cabin." Margaret Fuller brought her tragic moods into the house, where she spent the last evening before embarking with her son and husband on the voyage to America that was to end in shipwreck and death and cast gloom over the happiness in Casa Guidi.

Dickens, Thackeray and Hans Christian Andersen were visitors on their Italian journeyings. In a single day Story's little daughter was treated, in an effort to keep her quiet during an illness, to an authors' reading of rather more distinguished caliber than falls to the lot of most children. One after another the men of letters sat on the edge of her bed and laid before her their best wares. The great master of the fairy tale obliged with " The Ugly Duckling." Thackeray produced the as yet unpublished manuscript of " The Rose and the Ring," and Robert ended the session with " The Pied Piper of Hamelin."

William Page, " the American Titian," amused the adult circle for hours with his talk about the secrets of pigmentation which the great masters of the Renaissance had held. He was credited with having rediscovered many of these secrets, but the great stir he created in the world of art subsided quickly without leaving a trace, for there was one trick he had not learned, the formula for a paint that would remain bright. One by one his canvases turned black until their subjects were no longer recognizable. His portrait of Robert, which he presented to Ba and which she was not alone in considering a princely gift, faded gradually away and the painter's queer theories were speedily forgotten.

Page's arguments with Frederick Leighton, the Royal Academician, enlivened many a gathering in Florence and Rome, although it was seldom the two professionals had the field to themselves. Every one of their hearers entertained decided opinions on such matters and the debates waxed furious and general.

Hatty Hosmer, the Modern Woman of her day and " a favorite with both of us," as Ba wrote, amused the company with her extravagant independence. Hatty was pretty, twenty-two, had already quite a reputation as a sculptress and deserved it. Her little mannerisms and gestures of emancipation were regarded merely as the excusable follies of a wild American. She lived quite alone, without chaperon or elderly female relative of any kind, ate at cafes alone, rode horseback unescorted (until Rome's chief of police forbade the practice on the ground that the sight too much disturbed the equanimity of the citizenry). Yet despite these idiosyncrasies, respectable folk still spoke to her! Hatty was queer, they agreed, but she was a good girl. Her friends prided themselves on being broad-minded.

Between seasons in London, Kenyon descended upon Casa Guidi for a few weeks, beaming through his spectacles, tak-

ing great credit for the happiness of his friends and applauding their way of life.

Indeed, the masters of Casa Guidi proved to be such a contagious specimen of marital felicity that the timid Wilson surprised them by deciding to follow in her mistress's footsteps. She married Fernando, the Browning handy-man, thereby insuring the family perpetual possession of another devoted servant.

The death of Wordsworth in 1850 provided a pleasant debate in Florence over the proper poet to fill the vacant Laureateship. Ba's first choice was Robert, her second Leigh Hunt. Robert's first choice was Ba, his second Tennyson. He proved the more representative of the popular taste in both instances. In England Robert's name was never once mentioned for the post, but many critics thought a female Laureate would be eminently appropriate since England had a female sovereign.

" There is no living poet of either sex who can prefer a higher claim than Mrs. Elizabeth Barrett Browning," said the *Athenaeum,* taking the lead in urging her appointment.

" It won't be given to *me,* be sure, though the suggestion has gone the round of the English newspapers," she wrote when the reports from London were delivered in Italy.

She was quite right. The choice quickly narrowed to Tennyson and Leigh Hunt, and Tennyson was selected. The failure of the Brownings to interest the mass of the reading public and their long absence from England were responsible for their being passed over. Neither had received a publisher's check for a year, while Tennyson's royalties in the same period amounted to £500, a true index of relative popularity in 1850. "Christmas Eve and Easter Day," the first poem Robert published after his marriage, appeared that spring and sold two hundred copies in the first fortnight.

"After which," the poet recorded ruefully, "the demand flagged."

Over the sea came from "the verminous tribe," as Robert called all critics, harsh commentaries on the desertion of England by two of her leading poets. They answered the criticism by returning to London for the summer of 1851. Very cold, very foggy, physically very unpleasant, they found it. Tennyson offered them the use of his town house. Arnould, who was rising to leadership at the bar, offered them his home. They refused, and took gloomy, uncomfortable lodgings where Ba's cough returned. Robert, however, enjoyed mingling again in the old society. Once more he could indulge in long arguments with Carlyle on the advantages of being alive. Jane came to call, forgiving the damage to her rug so many years ago, and Ba discovered that probably the poor woman, "full of thought and feeling and character, it seems to me," might not be as responsible as Robert thought for her husband's tragic outlook on life.

Old Barrett took only sufficient notice of his daughter's

return to send the rest of his children out of town lest they
be contaminated by contact with the rebel. He rebuffed
wordlessly Robert's last move for a reconciliation and returned to him, unopened, all the letters Ba had written pleading for forgiveness. The rejected poets turned for comfort
to the society of Robert's father and sister. But for the
weather, their visit passed pleasantly enough, so pleasantly
that they were encouraged to return to London nearly every
summer that Ba's health would permit.

Tennyson sought them out and when his son, Hallam, was
christened, Robert proudly held the squirming infant in his
arms. Rossetti, too, was an admirer, and one evening the
Laureate came into town especially to read to them all passages from his new poem, " Maud." In his honor Robert
opened a second bottle of port after dinner and Tennyson,
thus stimulated, " opened his heart to us," and in a room un-
comfortably full of smoke read to the assembled guests not
merely extracts but the entire poem in his beautiful, booming voice. Overcome by his own powers, he paused at intervals to assure his audience, " There's a wonderful touch! "
or " That's very tender! " or even " How beautiful that is! "
It was half past two in the morning before he finished his
reading, and the listeners professed loudly to have enjoyed
it beyond all reason. Some of them, Ba and Robert for instance, were certainly sincere in their praise, and indeed the
evening had not been wasted. As Ba sat on the sofa beside

the reader, fuming at the chatter of some women who prevented her hearing all that Tennyson found so beautiful, Rossetti had retreated to a corner and before Tennyson finished " Maud," Rossetti had completed a rough pen and ink sketch of the poet.

In London, too, Mazzini came to see the Brownings, and they could talk for hours with the pale, unhealthy idealist about the future of Italy, the manifest destiny of free men, the creed of the believer in politics.

" I was thinking while he sat there," Ba wrote, " on what Italian turf he would lie at last with a bullet in his heart, or perhaps with a knife in his back, for to one of those ends it will surely come."

Florence Nightingale seemed a much less saintly figure, although the Brownings admired her " graceful manners " and the flowers that she sent. But Ba did not think her visitor was really doing much to make the world safe for women. Miss Nightingale, she said, was only a nurse, and nursing seemed to Ba to be rather a step backward for women who sought a place in the world of affairs.

The best part of any of the London visits was the breaking of the journey at Paris, the very queer Paris of Dumas and George Sand and Victor Hugo, the Paris that was still a medieval city but was about to become modern under the Second Empire and the genius of Haussmann. Ba and Robert managed to be in town for the most exciting of the

changes that raised an exile who had been for years considered a rather ridiculous figure to a brief career as master
of Europe by virtue of his uncle's name.

The poets hailed with the usual democratic cries of joy the
emergence of the Second Republic from the Commune of
'48. With millions of others, they believed in the words of
Prince Louis Napoleon, regarding him as he regarded himself, "the saviour of society." They did not realize that the
society which the new Bonaparte was saving was a blend
that united the harsh *régime* of Napoleon, minus its power
and glory, to the selfish commercialism of Louis Philippe,
without his peace and phlegm.

But the new President of France had spoken noble words
about Italy. He had reminded the peninsula in particular and
the world in general that his name was Bonaparte, and
Italian patriots remembered that it was an Italian name.
They remembered, too, the brief hopes of freedom which
had been inspired by Lodi and Castiglione and Arcola. Such
good Italians as the Brownings could not but wish well to
the man who aspired to refurbish these legends; such good
Englishmen as the Brownings were moved by the man's talk
of order and progress.

Robert, clear-sighted and shrewd in matters of European
politics, was disillusioned quickly, although Ba remained all
her life a passionate defender of the infinite goodness of her
hero. But her husband saw that Italy was not to be freed

as quickly as one might have inferred from the Prince-President's words, and, what was worse in the eyes of a confirmed liberal, France was not free either under the new rule.

> " A conservator, call me, if you please,
> Not a creator nor destroyer; one
> Who keeps the world safe."

This was the best plea Robert could put into the Prince's mouth when years later he attempted to explore the Imperial mind and set forth in " Prince Hohenstiel Schwangau " what he conceived to be the man's only possible justification. But in 1850, the poet's remarks were much plainer, if less worthy of the Browning reputation for keen psychological insight and involved phraseology.

" The President's an ass; he is not worth thinking of," Robert declaimed frequently when French politics were under discussion.

And of the other figures of the Second Republic he was equally critical.

" Thiers is a rascal; I make a point of not reading one word said by M. Thiers. Proudhon is a madman; who cares for Proudhon ? "

Ba did not share this contempt for the great men of France. She never lost her faith in the words of Louis Napoleon and while, during their Paris visits, they watched the anomaly

of a military tradition being resurrected from a muck of words, bourse speculation and banal scientific improvements, she grew ever more convinced that democracy was working through the strange instrumentality of a Bonaparte to accomplish its mysteriously delectable wonders. Their friends had opened to the Brownings some of the most popular, verbose and tiresome political salons in Paris, and as the men of the Republic wasted the shortening days of 1851 in interminable conversation, Ba and Robert watched with very different feelings the events that were leading up to the *coup d'etat*. Robert was suspicious and caustic; Ba confident and enthusiastic.

On the Second of December, the anniversary of Austerlitz, they woke up to learn that the Republican leaders were in jail or in flight and that a form of Government known as the Second Consulate had just been decreed in response to what the President pleased to call popular demand. A few hours later the poets stood at the windows of their apartment on the Champs-Élysées and were reminded of Leopold of Tuscany as Louis Napoleon rode past them at the head of a mighty escort, bowing receptively to cries of " Vive l'Empereur! " It was a far less tumultuous procession than the ones which had stirred them so deeply in Florence four years before, but Ba thought it a " grand spectacle " and would not have missed it for anything in the world. Robert muttered, a little surlily, something about breakers of oaths and fidelity to constitutions, but Ba took a more tolerant, more sentimental view.

" There was the army and the sun of Austerlitz and even I thought it one of the grandest of sights, for he rode there in the name of the people after all," she said.

It was just this last phrase that Robert doubted, and with justice. His wife entertained a gloriously naive faith in the sanctity and purity of plebiscites, but Robert could not help wondering just how free the voting really was.

" Robert and I have had some domestic émeutes because he hates some imperial names," Ba reported.

They argued about the great Napoleon and about the private life of the nephew. Robert did not believe in the public integrity of a man whose career was studded with as many amours as gossip credited, not without some foundation, to Louis Napoleon. Ba did not see what that had to do with it. Robert reasoned that a man who would violate an oath to the Constitution of the Republic could not be trusted to keep an oath to any other document. Ba retorted that he had broken only " the husk of an oath," but had been faithful to the intentions of the people.

She heard men say admiringly, " C'est le vrai neveu de son oncle! " and she agreed with them. Robert agreed too, but he also adhered to the party which was calling the uncle " le plus grand scélérat du monde." Husband and wife finally agreed to disagree. Robert continued to abuse the Prince and

Ba to defend him. She could not forget the sight of the impassive man, his trim figure tightly encased in an ornate uniform, trotting at the head of his troops to swing open a door " to a wider and calmer political liberty than France has yet enjoyed." Besides, Ba, as a connoisseur of whiskers, was fascinated by the neat imperial and the vast extravagance of the rolled and twisted Napoleonic moustache.

Even the mournful Thursday, when the only real protest against the *coup d'état* ran out in blood behind the barricades, did not shake Ba's faith in the new dictator. All night she and Robert sat up, listening to the rattle of musketry and the duller roar of the cannon. They were too far away to hear the screams of the dying, but Robert thought the dozens of lives crushed with the barricades which the army had mysteriously allowed to rise unmolested (one remembered then that the uncle had sprung to fame by mowing down the rioters of Paris) were a steep price to pay for the satisfaction of any one man's ambition.

The revolution, however, had not interfered with their routine. The baby was taken for his walk, Ba had her constitutional as usual, and one day all three drove out to see the shot-scarred walls, shattered windows and torn up streets where the barricades had been. After that, Ba assured her friends in England, all was well with the strange new liberalism in France.

" Everything is perfectly tranquil in Paris. On Sunday the

theaters were as full as usual and our Champs-Élysées had quite its complement of promenaders. Wiedemann's prophecy had not been carried out any more than the prophecies of the wiser may — the soldiers had not shot Punch."

No one doubted, however, that Punch would soon be Emperor. He was already accorded all the honors of royalty, and the shouts of "Vive l'Empereur!" were not confined to the Second of December. A discreetly encouraged agitation for the Empire swelled to nobly artificial proportions since it appeared that the Dictator was conferring upon his people the blessings of prosperity, and in November of 1852 Ba and Robert saw another procession along the Champs-Élysées. The new Emperor was riding through the streets again to display himself to the electorate which had just confirmed his title.

"He showed his usual tact and courage by riding on horseback quite alone, at least ten paces between himself and his nearest escort, which of course had a striking effect, taking the French on their weak side," Ba wrote.

Fortunately it was not all politics and "domestic émeutes" in Paris. Ba, the great romance reader, would have found the city delightful if for no other reason than that it was there she met the "inspired Negro child," Alexandre Dumas.

"If he has twenty sous and wants bread," she described him, "he buys a pretty cane instead. For the rest, 'bon enfant,' kind and amiable."

She and Robert plunged into the dizzy vortex of the immoral Parisian bohemia. Both of them felt extremely " advanced " when Robert, having perused " Diane de Lys," cried out:

" You must read that, Ba. It is clever, only outrageous as to morals."

But morals were thrown completely to the dogs in this gay Paris. Robert took his wife to see the frightfully improper but popular play, " La Dame aux Camélias," which was in the midst of its record breaking hundred nights' run. Robert wept without shame, although as a playwright himself he " gives himself out for blasé on dramatic matters."

" It almost broke my heart and split my head," said Ba, and added:

" Didn't I tell you how there were caricatures on the boulevards showing the public of the pit holding up umbrellas to protect themselves from the tears rained down by the public of the boxes? How the President of the Republic went to see, and sent a bracelet to the first actress, and how the English newspapers called him immoral for it? How I went to see myself, and how my aunt called me immoral for it? She 'quite wondered how Mr. Browning could allow such a thing,' not comprehending that Mr. Browning never, or scarcely ever, does think of restraining his wife from anything she pleases to do."

Even "La Dame aux Camelias" was not the worst. Some of their friends shook their heads in scandalized sorrow when they learned that the Brownings had actually called upon George Sand, not once, but twice. Really, that was a little over the odds. But the Brownings were defiant. They defended with spirit the propriety of communing with a genius even if she were not chaste, even if the society of her salon was vulgar, even if the brazen hussy did smoke.

As a matter of fact, Ba risked her health to drive out, bundled in furs on a raw, wet April day, to visit the great Frenchwoman who had so kindly asked the English poets to call. She was disappointed in not seeing her hostess smoke, was surprised at the quiet simplicity of the woman's manners and was disgusted by the shameless indecency with which her more ardent admirers kissed her hand, and right out before everybody, too. But Ba agreed with Robert that the visits were well worth while, all the more so that their new acquaintance sent them tickets to her new play, "Les Vacances de Pandolphe," which turned out to be as great a failure as anything Robert himself had ever written.

He saw more of Madame Sand than his wife, for he called several times when Ba was too ill to go with him. He also walked with the novelist in the Tuileries Gardens, and indulged in improving conversation with the greatest woman

of the day. He was genuinely pleased to think that she was a greater genius and less immoral than people thought. Both he and Ba, however, agreed that he had displayed the acme of tolerance in permitting his wife to mingle, even for a moment, in the low company of the Sand salon.

THIRTEEN

THE GOLDEN DAYS

LONDON with its great men and old friends, Paris with its excitements and revolutions could never hold the Brownings long from Italy. Always they returned with sighs of relief to Casa Guidi, to the sunsets on the Arno, to the gossip and excursions of their circle. They were glad, too, to get back to the material comforts of a home. In London and Paris Robert found it necessary to quarrel about their lodgings with the owners. All London rooms were so dark and cold. Paris apartments which were splendid in yellow satin furniture were unable to provide hot water. At Casa Guidi they had room and air and light and the devoted ministrations of Wilson and Fernando.

Also there were friends for the little Penini. As the boy grew, his parents found a new vocation, that of teacher. Robert was very regular in his instructions, having undertaken the bulk of his son's education, and was learning to be strict. Music and arithmetic, his own strong points, were his chief contribution to Pen's accomplishments, while Ba helped the boy prepare his lessons and read German with him. The parents were very proud that the child already prattled with equal ease and volume in English, French and Italian, and had acquired a most charming manner when passing tea and cakes to his elders.

They were not, however, neglecting their own work. Ba's " Aurora Leigh " and Robert's " Men and Women " came out almost together, the wife Browning's work far over-shadowing that of the husband Browning in popularity, as one critic expressed it. Robert was delighted. His early sen-sitiveness to adverse criticism had been calloused by much buffeting, and any attacks on himself went unnoticed in his rejoicing at the praise showered upon Ba. " Aurora Leigh " made a great and immediate hit and went into a second edition within a fortnight. Robert made a collection of all the reviews. He would pull them out of his pocket in all sorts of company and read them with great expression and gusto until forcibly restrained.

Ba was not nearly so set up as he about her success. She was bitter about the stupidity of a public which preferred her work to " Men and Women." In themselves, the fifty poems were, she vowed, the finest that ever came from mortal pen. Of the fifty-first she could say nothing. For the fifty-first was " One Word More," and under the dedication " To E. B. B." was Robert's reply to " Sonnets from the Portu-guese." She nearly burst with pride as, after nearly nine years of married life, she read Robert's cry of love from its beginning:

> " Take them, Love, the book, and me together.
> Where the heart lies, let the brain lie also."

through the two hundred lines of ever increasing tenderness to the end:

> " Oh, their Rafael of the dear Madonnas,
> Oh, their Dante of the dread Inferno,
> Wrote one song — and in my brain I sing it,
> Drew one angel — borne, see, on my bosom! "

That such a book, so dedicated, should meet with anything short of universal adulation seemed monstrous. But Carlyle, writing with the frankness of old friendship, explained just why the work failed so conspicuously of the reception Ba had envisaged for it.

" My friend," he told Robert, " it is what they call ' unintelligibility! ' That is a fact; you are dreadfully difficult to understand; and that is really a sin. Admit the accusation; I testify to it. God knows I too understand very well what it is to be ' unintelligible ' so called. It is the effort of a man with very much to say endeavoring to get it said in a not sordid or unworthy way to men who are at home chiefly in the sordid, the prosaic, inane and unworthy."

But the sage of Chelsea was not blind to the beauty of his

friend's work. Carlyle had a sneaking respect for poetry, which he kept pretty well disguised under a cutting habit of speech. His own favorite verse was " Charlie is My Darling." He could, and did, wax eloquent over the interpretation of the Scotch ballad:

> " Gie me but my lass
> I care not for my cogie."

Quite seriously he would explain that the singer was willing to give up drink for his girl. And once, with an appealing look in Jane's direction, the old prince of pessimists had said:

" Some day in spite of my nature and my stars I shall burst into a song."

So now he ended his letter of admonition with a bit of encouragement for the man who had been devoting nearly twenty-five years to serving Euterpe.

" I do not," he conceded, " at this point any longer forbid you verse, as probably I once did."

The poet complained that a great deal of the obscurity was due to typographical errors. He sent Rossetti a list of sixteen corrections that were essential to an understanding of the text, but even then his meaning escaped certain critics. Of " Bishop Blougram's Apology," admittedly designed for Cardinal Wiseman, whose wit and learning were the delight of Catholic drawing rooms, whose work among the poor was winning converts, but whose showy magnificence based on the splendors of Rome had raised a new cry of " No Popery " in England, the author said:

" But there is nothing hostile about it."

His Eminence must have misunderstood the poet's meaning. He himself wrote a review of the poem for the *Rambler,* a Catholic journal, and in it could be discerned a certain resentment at being characterized as one who sought Church preferment because

" There's a power in me and will to dominate
    Which I must exercise, they hurt me else:
    In many ways I need mankind's respect,
    Obedience, and the love that's born of fear:
    While at the same time, there's a taste I have,
    A toy of soul, a titillating thing,
    Refuses to digest these dainties crude.
    The naked life is gross till clothed upon:
    I must take what men offer, with a grace
    As though I would not, could I help it, take!
    An uniform I wear though over-rich —
    Something imposed on me, no choice of mine;
    No fancy-dress worn for pure fancy's sake
    And despicable therefore! now folk kneel
    And kiss my hand — of course the Church's hand.
    Thus I am made, thus life is best for me,
    And thus that it should be I have procured;

And thus it could not be another way.
I venture to imagine."

Wiseman was more generous than most of the professional reviewers and admitted that the poem, "though ut-
terly mistaken in the very groundwork of religion, though
starting from the most unworthy notions of the work of a
Catholic Bishop, and defending a self-indulgence every
honest man must feel to be disgraceful, is yet in its way
triumphant." The Cardinal vindicated thus the reputation
for sound artistic appreciation which the world and the poet
gave him. But critics, editors, publishers, booksellers and
readers were all very far away, and Robert could say with
his own Andrea del Sarto:

"I, painting from myself and to myself,
    Know what I do, am unmoved by men's blame
    Or their praise either."

In Florence there was ample compensation for any cool-
ness that might exist in England. Ba rejoiced that their
bachelor friends came to Casa Guidi without formality or
restraint and were so kind as to include her in their discussions. It was pleasant, too, to arrange these impromptu
gatherings after the elaborate preparations and invitations
so necessary in London.

Ticknor and Fields, the Boston publishers, fell victims to a strange generosity, whose only precedent had been Ba's ten per cent. in 1845, and sent Robert a check for some of his poems which they had printed. It was a unique event in the history of literature, and they celebrated with an elaborate picnic to which all their friends came, rejoicing at the chance of helping to spend such an unexpected windfall.

They all agreed that even the Grand Duke's ball was less princely. They went to the ball, however, and Ba so far entered into the spirit of the carnival as to flirt outrageously from under her mask. The excitement tired her quickly and she went home early, but Robert remained until dawn, also flirting, and came away at last, marvelling that so much gayety on the part of the lower classes could be so orderly. All Florence was wandering in and out of the Palace, Fernando jostling the Grand Duke in the ballroom and free on this one night to wink at noble ladies, but there was no rioting or other unseemly conduct that, Robert said, would have attended a similar experiment in England. For the Brownings such gayeties were rare. More usual were the quiet evenings at home or at the homes of friends.

" There were quantities of talk, controversy and confidences, evening after evening," Ba wrote. " Mr. Lytton had a reception on the terrace of his villa at Bellosguardo the evening before our last in Florence and we were all bachelors together there, and I made tea and we ate strawberries

and cream and talked spiritualism through one of the pleas-
antest two hours that I remember. Such a view! Florence
dissolving in the purple of the hills; and the stars looking on.
Mr. Tennyson was there, Mr. Powers, and Senator Villari, an
accomplished Sicilian, besides our young host and ourselves.
How we 'set down' Faraday for his 'arrogant and insolent
letter' (a scientific attack on spiritualism) and what stories
we told, and what miracles we swore to! Oh, we are be-
lievers here, except Robert, who persists in wearing a coat of
respectable scepticism — so considered — though it is much
out of elbows and ragged about the skirts."

This business of communications with the dead was becoming of increasing importance in the Browning household. Ever since her young womanhood, Ba had nourished
an absorbing interest in spiritualism and had solaced the
pain of illness and grief with her faith in the possibilities of
speech with the dead. She was singularly credulous, although
professing to believe only in " authenticated phenomena."
But she could never shake Robert's crass "respectable
scepticism."

" The difference between me and the stupid people who
have 'communications' is probably nothing more than that
I don't confound the results of the natural working of what
is in my mind," he said, but thinking that might be a little
harsh towards Ba he added, "I am never angry with the
purely duped."

He was, however, frequently angry with those who, in his opinion, were deceiving his friends as a means of making a living. He was particularly bitter about Daniel Home, the most impudent of the mediums who visited Casa Guidi. Home, who devoted his life to preying upon the hopes and fears of the gullible, found Ba an unusually easy mark for his tricks. He so worked upon her feelings that Robert, having exposed the man's favorite trick of spitting blood while in a trance, forbade her attendance at any more of his seances, for she usually emerged from them in such a state of nervous exhaustion that she was ill for days. She thought her husband quite wrong, but did not think of questioning his authority. Indeed, she accepted his prohibition so as a matter of right that later she reported his yielding to the point of letting her have the *Spiritual Magazine* from England as a singularly benevolent and kindly act.

Also, Robert never interfered with her discussion of the spirits as long as the ghostly voices were not marshalled by a professional, and Ba's store of " authenticated communications " was swelled constantly by the tales of the intimates of Casa Guidi. Mrs. Stowe especially provided material for the triumphant vindication of Ba's faith, for the novelist was able to record frequent conversations with her son who had been killed during a hazing incident at college.

On political questions the Brownings were more in accord. As a British army struggled with its allies in the cold

mud of the Crimea, as the casualty lists lengthened and the inevitable administrative scandals that attend all wars crept into public knowledge, Robert proclaimed vigorously that the Ministry should be torn limb from limb. He was annoyed that Englishmen should be so stupid as the Government seemed, for he took it as a personal affront to himself as an Englishman. He had quite a good time at Liberal parties in London that summer, however, abusing the Ministry. Ba was equally interested and equally enraged.

"If our people had never had to pay for an army," she wrote, "they might sit down quietly under the taunt of wanting experience. But we have soldiers, and soldiers should have military education as well as red coats and be led by properly qualified officers instead of Lord Nincompoop's youngest sons. As it is in the army, so it is in the State. Places given away, here and there, to incompetent heads; nobody being responsible, no unity of idea and purpose anywhere — the individual interest always in the way of the general good."

The war, however, did not otherwise interfere with them. They continued their round of travels about Italy, journeying with great luxury from Florence to Rome in a private carriage lent them by an American admirer, Mr. Eckley. The coachman was not very skillful and nearly killed them. Twice they were delayed for some time while the peasantry pulled them out of ditches. On this trip Robert became involved in the only brawl of his career. Two ox drivers whose teams blocked the road were quarreling about who was to blame, and as the Browning carriage rolled up one of the disputants pulled a knife. Robert, with his horror of civil disorder, leaped from his seat and rushed between the fighters. In a moment all three were in a tangle of swinging arms and Ba screamed as the knife described wide, shining arcs above her husband's head. But in a moment the still athletic poet had pushed the drivers apart and emerged from the fray with no other damage than a pair of torn trousers which embarrassed him frightfully all the rest of the day.

After the publication of "Men and Women," Robert dropped into protracted idleness. He decided to try his hand at sculpture and spent many hours in Story's studio modelling with much enthusiasm and but little skill. Ba's attempts to draw him back to literary effort were fruitless; he said he had nothing to say at the moment and did not care about writing just to be setting words on paper. He was quite content to act as tutor to his son and critic to his wife.

The cool reception England was according his last book could not be responsible for his indolence, for he was acquiring for the first time a considerable public. Americans, who had long been reading Ba's works, were now buying in great numbers those of her husband. They and the more

enlightened Englishmen were also seeking out autographs of the author. Dozens of his public turned up wherever he might be and explained that they were only in search of a few lines of his own poetry written in his own hand. With immense quantities of doggerel, which he was very fond of quoting and originating, and with volumes of other men's serious poetry stored up in his head, Robert was quite unable to remember just how his own verses ran. At last the requests became so numerous and so impossible to refuse that he deliberately memorized one of his own shorter pieces, and from that time on the autograph books of his acquaintances were filled with:

> " All that I know
>> Of a certain star
> Is, it can throw
>> (Like the angled spar)
> Now a dart of red,
>> Now a dart of blue;
> Till my friends have said
>> They would fain see too,
> My star that dartles the red and the blue.
> Then it stops like a bird; like a flower hangs furled:
>> They must solace themselves with the Saturn above it.
> What matter to me if their star is a world?
>> Mine has opened its soul to me; therefore I love it."

The appreciation of men and women, mostly women, who sought such trifles did not seem to Ba to be sufficient.

"The blindness, deafness and stupidity of the English public to Robert are amazing," she complained. "As a lion Robert has his range in society, and for the rest you should see Chapman's returns: while in America he's a power, a writer, a poet. He is read — he lives in the hearts of the people. 'Browning readings' here in Boston. 'Browning evenings' there. For the rest, the English hunt lions too, but their favorite lions are chosen among 'lords' chiefly or 'railroad kings.' 'It's worth eating much dirt,' said an Englishman of high family and character here, 'to get to Lady ——'s soiree.' Americans will eat dirt to get to *us.* English people will come to stare at *me* sometimes, but physicians, dentists, who serve me and refuse their fees, artists who give me pictures, friends who give up their carriages and make other practical sacrifices are *not English.*"

There was, however, no longer any need at all of considering the financial aspect of their work. The Browning income now far exceeded the Browning expenses, for their tastes remained as simple as ever. Ba's poetry was selling very well again, leading her to express the opinion that on the whole their art paid better than novel writing. But the biggest part of their prosperity after 1856 was the fruit of friendship. Kenyon died that year and left the Brownings £11,000, which in itself provided an income amply suffi-

cient for the family requirements and even stretched to include a pony for Penini. Ba's father died a few months later, and Robert had determined that his wife might accept nothing from the estate of the man who had cast them off with such marked discourtesy. The resolution was not put to the test. Old Barrett did not mention them in his will.

His death cast only a very small cloud over Casa Guidi. It was not within even Ba's power to mourn very deeply or ostentatiously for the man who had sentenced her to death to satisfy his caprice. She had resented it a little, and rather perversely, that he had seemed in his last years quite as happy as before she ran away. At least so her sisters wrote, and it was characteristic enough to excite little surprise in anyone less determined than Ba to minimize his faults. But the final alienation had been due to the rigid disciplinarian's disrespectful rejection of Robert's advances. Disrespect to Robert was the unforgivable offense.

So there was nothing in his death to prevent their having quite a gay season in Rome, where Robert resumed his youthful habit of going out of an evening. He always stayed at home for dinner and was never gone all night, but he no longer declined all evening engagements which Ba did not want to accept with him. Indeed, he frequently had two or three parties scheduled for the same evening, and went to them all, with disastrous results to his work.

"No men and women," Ba lamented, but she was glad to see him enjoy himself, and she was genuinely proud to add: "The women adore him everywhere too much for decency. Dissipations decidedly agree with Robert, there's no denying that, though he's horribly hypocritical and ' prefers an evening with me at home,' which has grown to be a kind of dissipation also."

Occasionally Robert even invaded the Italian bohemia and was immensely gratified to be recognized there. The pleasantly informal custom of poetic contests still prevailed in a Rome which was ignorant of football, and one night in a cafe as two champions sat across from each other prepared to declaim impromptu verses at a critical audience, a workman at an adjoining table adjured them in fantastically flowery address to outdo themselves this night for no other than the distinguished English poet, Signor Roberto Browning, was listening.

Even gayer evenings were not unknown. Late one night Robert and his friends emerged from a lengthy contemplation of the wine in its reddest state, inspired to a tuneful and extravagant mood. With a band of hired musicians in one cab and themselves in another, they drove through the quiet streets of Rome roaring defiantly all those patriotic airs which the Pope had ordered must not be sung aloud in his States. The revellers went singing happily until a sight of the Papal police trotting around a corner dampened their patriotic ardor, and they changed their tune hastily under the suspicious glances of the watch.

It was in Rome, too, that Robert had his first contact with English royalty and felt his honest English heart enlarge in his bosom at the pride of the meeting. He was within a month of his forty-seventh birthday; his beard had gone almost completely white and his head quite gray in the service of his muse; his works had placed him, other writers agreed, on the top of the poetic heap with only Tennyson and Hunt and possibly his own wife to dispute absolute supremacy; a group of devoted admirers was foreshadowing the homage of the future Browning Societies, but this command to dine with the young Albert Edward, Prince of Wales, was the highest honor he had yet earned by his pen.

Under the careful tutelage of Colonel Bruce, the Prince was making the first of his foreign tours, and the men he met — it was no part of the plan to expose him to feminine companionship — were most carefully selected. The invitation to Robert was as much a tribute to the poet's well-known respectability and learning as to his genius.

"It will gratify the Queen that the Prince should make the acquaintance of Mr. Browning," said Colonel Bruce in issuing the royal command, which did not include Ba only because of the orders from Windsor that Bertie should not move in mixed society.

There was a great stir in the Browning apartment on the

day set for the interview between the royal stripling and the mature poet-philosopher. For once Ba was afraid Robert might not acquit himself in the brilliant manner she desired for him. She hovered about him, giving good advice and telling him what to say and what to avoid saying. Robert's good-natured tactlessness when he essayed flattery was a standing joke among their friends. He had once with great gusto thanked Emelyn Story for a pleasant visit with a very cheerful: "I had a delightful evening. I never spoke to you once." And to a painter mournfully deploring his own dissatisfaction with his work, Robert had said in a tone meant to soothe and encourage, "But my dear fellow, if you were satisfied, you would be so very easily satisfied."

"So I exhorted my Robert to eschew compliments and keep to Italian politics," Ba wrote in describing the honor paid to the family, and at last she sent him off, dignified, handsome and splendid in his best clothes, to convert Albert Edward to the ideals that animated Italian patriots.

Robert did his best. The Prince and his entourage were so relieved to find that Mr. Browning did not speak in the obscure blank verse of his more difficult poems that they encouraged him to speak of politics and avoid literature. As a poet, Robert could go further than any politician in outlining the helpful rôle he would like to see England take. He spent a genuinely pleasant evening in the same sort of talk as was common when he foregathered with friends in his

own home. He was well pleased with himself, and hurried back to assure Ba that he had comported himself with the greatest decorum, had presented Italy's case with all the eloquence at his command.

As for the Prince — "He is a gentle, refined boy," said Robert.

Albert Edward, with the tact impressed upon him from earliest youth, refrained from expressing any recorded opinion of his visitor.

FOURTEEN

WAR AND POLITICS

ROBERT'S conversation with His Royal Highness had no appreciable effect on England's policy in Italy. In fact Her Majesty's Government seemed to the Brownings to be vying with Prussia in an inimical coldness to the rights of man. The name of Cavour was beginning to replace that of Mazzini in their list of heroes. Soon they were arguing that the only possible saviours of Italy were Garibaldi and the round bespectacled, astute politician at Victor Emmanuel's elbow — and of course, Ba added, Napoleon. The poor idealist in London and his dreams of republics counted for less than nothing in their calculations. The Brownings maintained stoutly that they were done with mere words.

From the vantage point of Rome they watched the careful goading of Austria, but they were back in Florence to celebrate the triumph of arms as Napoleon in person led the armies of the Empire to a victory over Austria on the plains of Lombardy. A huge French flag flew before Casa Guidi beside the Italian colors. Within the house, the Brownings were

crying out against the cowardice of England which some-
how failed to follow the noble example of France. The
British Ministry, indeed, was regarding the fine French
gesture with a sceptical eye.

The victories at Magenta and Solferino, however, uplifted
the poets above all such minor considerations as British policy, for a few days. With the Austrians in full flight, or at
least so all good Italians believed, even Robert began to
suspect that Napoleon might be sincere. But before he could
commit himself to any rash praises, they heard that peace
had been made at Villafranca and Italy had not been given
the fruits of victory. Napoleon had remembered that besides bearing an Italian name he was Emperor of the
French. He knew, too, that Magenta and Solferino had
not been victories in the true Napoleonic sense, for they
had not convinced the enemy that he was really beaten
and had not convinced his own armies that they were in-
vincible.

In Florence for just one day every portrait, every bust,
every medal of the Emperor, and they had adorned thousands of windows and walls, disappeared into dark boxes
and drawers as people murmured mysteriously of betrayal
and French perfidy. Men protested that the whole war had
been merely a Napoleonic plot to acquire Savoy and Nice
from a gullible Piedmont while the Emperor pretended to be
a friend of freedom. The French flag no longer flew at Casa

Guidi, and Ba was crying out in verse that echoed the spirited anger of her circle:

" Peace, peace, peace do you say?
    What! — with the enemy's guns in our ears?
    With the country's wrongs not rendered back?
What! — While Austria stands at bay
    In Mantua, and our Venice bears
    The cursed flag of the yellow and black? "

The cry of sorrow which Victor Emmanuel had thought he heard arising from his country had not died, but after the one day it was no longer directed against Napoleon. The medals, busts and portraits returned to their accustomed places, but the French flag was not restored at Casa Guidi. The Brownings had gone to Siena where Robert admired the view and began to worry a great deal about Ba's health. There was cause for worry. The excitement of politics, the disappointment of Villafranca, the fierce debates and the unrestrained passion she put into her arguments were bringing a return of the London cough.

At Siena she was very sick. Dr. Gresonowsky, a Prussian physician with Italian sympathies, who refused to accept a fee for his ministrations, followed them to Siena as much for the pleasure of helping Ba abuse Prussia and England as for the professional attentions he was able to bestow. Rob-

"OUR DEGRADED DRAMA."

Tense Moment in a Stage Hit of the Early 'Forties.

ert was very grateful, so grateful that he did not intrude his own opinion of Napoleon into the discussion, especially as nearly all the English doctors had fled from Italy during the war and Gresonowsky agreed with Ba.

When he wanted to express his own views he went to see Landor, who at eighty-five was still regarding his protégé of nearly fifty as quite a promising young man of whom the world would yet hear. The fortune that had permitted Landor's indulgence in satire and expensive enthusiasms for half a century had been dissipated at last, and the old man, hating the world with a bitterness that is only engendered by domestic troubles, had sought the refuge of his friends. Robert was one of the few who could forgive the violent outbursts of suspicion and ingratitude with which Landor repaid the kindest attentions.

"I take care of him," the younger poet explained simply, "his amiable family having clawed him a little too sharply. I mean his Fiesole 'family,' a trifle of wife, sons and daughters."

Landor's brothers, however, proved more adequate than the wife who had driven a husband old enough to be her father from the house. They refused to have anything to do with the famous member of the family if he dared come back to England, but they were willing to make him a comfortable allowance as long as he remained in Italy. Robert was grateful to them for their forbearance, and tended his

one time patron with an assiduity that led his wife to refer to the old man as " Robert's adopted son."

Lodgings were found for Landor near the Brownings whether they were at Casa Guidi or in Siena. Wilson was sent over to take care of him and Robert loyally spent a great deal of time assuring the old man that it was not necessarily a sign of being poisoned that he occasionally was obliged to cling to the rail while going down stairs. Other men of eighty-five often sought such support, Robert said gravely. To distract these quite groundless fears, Robert helped heap opprobrium upon the unconscious head of the French Emperor. When Landor grew restive even at that happy pastime and began to recite the catalogue of his own woes, Robert soothed his friend by quoting (with appropriately admiring comments) from the works of Walter Savage Landor. That never failed.

" The poor old lion is very quiet on the whole," Ba wrote, " roaring softly to beguile the time in awful Latin alcaics, to say nothing of hexameters and pentameters, against his wife and Louis Napoleon. Such an extraordinary union of great literary gifts and incapacity of will has seldom surprised the world."

But Ba could forgive him anything. He had believed in Robert's genius years ago and besides,

" He has the most beautiful sea-foam of a beard you ever saw, all in a curl and white bubblement of beauty."

Despite Ba's assurances, however, not all the old lion's roars were soft. When he had taken an idea that he was being poisoned, his custom was to hurl the dinner, dishes and all, out of the window. He was still strong enough to break the furniture and terrorize poor Wilson.

"I suppose," Robert admitted, "Mr. Landor plagues and frightens her; a grasshopper's is the stouter soul of the two."

And a little later:

"I have heard from Landor and Wilson. All is going well enough, only he is teasing to have the house altered, windows made, the terrace extended to the garden, rather inconsistently with his expressed conviction of not outliving another year."

Very gently Robert, as custodian of the poet's allowance from England, resisted these whims. Only the old man's persistent quarrels with his wife and children stirred the younger man's criticism to a note of harshness. Otherwise he was able to chronicle the annoyances for which Landor was responsible and add with cheerful tolerance, "Bless him!" But the strong Browning family feeling was aroused by the sight and sound of the Landor "domestic émeutes," and he commented rather severely:

"So demeans himself in his sad old age one of the greatest geniuses England ever produced."

For the rest, Robert was able to derive amusement from the hypochondriac's really excellent health. The most learned poet of his day exercised his talent for doggerel at his aged friend's expense and set down gleefully such bits of household information as:

"The plate was large, the eggs were four.
He breakfasted, there was no more!"

When Robert called Landor would sometimes produce a new epitaph he had written for himself, usually in Latin and always rather flowery. The visitor would admire the beauty of the verse while deploring the sentiment. He could not realize that for years Landor had been really enjoying the thought of death and that it was this lugubrious pleasure that led him to insist that the title pages of his new books should bear the legend, "By the late W. S. Landor." His younger friend felt that this must be a pose, but he did not know just what kind.

"Whatever he may profess," said Robert, "the thing he really loves is a pretty girl to talk nonsense with, and he finds comfort in American visitors who hold him in proper respect."

It was a preference Robert could appreciate. He too liked to talk at a pretty face, and his American friends held him in that proper respect which he knew Landor found so gratifying.

While the two poets abused Napoleon to their hearts' content and Ba and Dr. Gresonowsky took out their spleen

in reviling their native countries, they were all four finding
the shock of Villafranca subsiding in the discovery that
Italy might actually free herself without foreign interven-
tion. As Leopold fled forever from Tuscany and the "Iron
Baron," Bettino Ricasoli, undertook a dictatorship which
was to end only in union with Piedmont, the Brownings
prepared to collaborate on an Italian piece, their only attempt
at joint production. But their views on that subject were so
divergent after the peace that Robert withdrew from the
undertaking and left Ba to write "Poems Before Congress" alone. He went on with his modelling, while she
quite let herself go. She had no doubts about the reception
her work would receive.

"I expect," she said, "to be torn to pieces by English critics
for what I have ventured to write."

She was not mistaken. The cry was so loud and the conviction of her disloyalty to the purity of British motives so
widespread that when she wrote "A Curse for a Nation,"
the denunciation of the expatriate poetess attained such
fierceness that even Ba was amazed at "that mob of 'Saturday reviewers' who take their mud and their morals from
the same place and use voices hoarse with hooting down
English poetesses to cheer on the English champion, Tom
Sayers." The redoubtable Tom, heavyweight champion of
the world, was just then training for his immortal victory
over Heenan, an event which led Ba to exclaim:

"They subscribed five thousand pounds in England for Tom Sayers. There's the advance of civilization!"

However, the reviewers were not altogether at fault. When Ba wrote "A Curse for a Nation," she thought she was directing it quite obviously at the United States and slavery. She was ever a timely writer and the year was 1860. England would have applauded the sentiment, but unfortunately English readers did not know what she was talking about, a fate to which it was difficult for the Brownings to resign themselves. In view of "Poems Before Congress," it was quite natural to assume, as even the mild Henrietta and the learned *Athenaeum* did, that the "Curse" was directed against England and her Italian policy. Apparently America put the same interpretation upon it, for the only result of the "Curse" across the Atlantic was a most flattering offer of $100 for every piece Mrs. Browning cared to contribute, even though it were as short as a sonnet, and that for the magazine rights alone.

Robert attributed the misinterpretation of Ba's poem to the sheer malevolence of "the verminous tribe." They ought to know without being told, he contended, that his wife was interested in other politics besides the Italian. With so many American friends it was natural that the Brownings should watch closely the preparations for civil war.

Their natural sympathies with the North were bolstered by the fact that most of their friends came from Massachu-

setts. They were confirmed in their opinion by meeting Charles Sumner, who was vainly seeking in Europe the health which Brooks' cane had beaten out of him. His stoicism under the tortures which his ingenious physicians devised to make his last days miserable won the Brownings' admiration. They spared a few thoughts from Garibaldi's Neapolitan campaign to pray that there would be no compromise over slavery. As liberals, the Brownings demanded the sturdy maintenance of principle, no matter what the cost in American blood.

When they went to Rome, they had little time for American troubles. For here they lived the life of conspirators and gloried in it. They were being more and more sought after by travelers, but they avoided their countrymen for the society of obscure Italian patriots who thronged the apartment, threadbare and noisy and full of secrets, side by side with men who knew the real secrets, walked quietly and talked softly. For such men as the first class, the Brownings maintained a sort of café. Thanks to the French general, Comte de Noue, who was upholding the Papal authority at the head of French troops, the Brownings received seditious newspapers which the Pope had banned from his domains. The journals came addressed to the General himself, for no one dared tamper with his mail, and in return for his courtesy, the real recipients refrained from speaking about it. At all hours of the day or night, meanwhile, the friends of liberty dropped in to see the Brownings and read the news. Most of them were friends, too, of Fernando. They were afraid to carry the journals away lest they be caught harboring such incriminating documents, and so they became the nucleus of the " Café Browning."

Here Garibaldi's victories were fought over and over again. Cavour's words, or what men said were Cavour's words, were repeated. The confidences of mysterious, perhaps mythical, men in high places were guardedly violated.

And Robert resolutely refused to do any work. He spent four hours a day in Story's studio, but not a word would be put on paper. He could not bring himself to write while Ba was enduring the discomfort of her old cough. They left Rome in search of health for her, but neither Florence nor Siena could give it to her now. She was artificially sustained only by drugs and the excitement of politics and war. Tuscany under the rule of the " Iron Baron " was sadly disorganized, and on the Exchange the bonds which the new Government had floated were dropping steadily. Robert had invested heavily in these issues. Now in defiance of all advice and of his own severely practical instincts, he plunged even more deeply into the falling market. It was to be his sacrifice for Italy, and he was more than repaid by Ba's applause.

"Robert, generally so timid in such things," she wrote

proudly, " has caught a flush of my rashness, and is alarmed neither by sinking funds nor rising loans."

In the end his rashness paid dividends. He was in effect gambling on a united Italy, and he did not have to wait long before the game was won. It was eminently fitting that his only outburst of that financial madness which was supposed to characterize all poets should have turned out to be profitable. Even in his madness he could not commit follies which his financier ancestors might have regarded with disapproval as bad business.

But he did another and even better stroke of business in Florence, thanks to the habit which he had copied from his father of never passing a book-shop without stepping inside, no matter how mean it might appear, to investigate the oldest rags of forgotten volumes. Only that habit, and, he said, the heat outside, led him into the unpromising little hole on the Piazza San Lorenzo, and even when he emerged with a battered little volume, part manuscript and part print, he did not realize what an excellent investment he had made. But as he went about telling his friends the story of the Roman murder case which the little book contained, he conceived the notion that a man might write as well as tell such a story.

Crime had always been one of his absorbing interests. With the fascination of a tabloid addict, he pored over newspaper accounts of the latest murders. They could not come

too gory for his taste. He never tired of pondering the complex emotions which provoked the shedding of blood. And why was the murder committed in just that way? he always wondered. The little yellow book from Florence was a chance to show how a murder story should be told, a splendidly theatrical skein of gorgeous settings, picturesque brutality, lusty rage, devilish slyness, outraged virtue, ostentatious purity, cloying sweetness, all soaked in blood, plenty of blood, and all to be woven together and bound with a shrewd exposure of the workings of the human mind upon human passions. It was worth thinking about, and Robert was prepared to think for a long time.

He was not prepared to write, but Ba was. The critical reception of "Poems Before Congress" could not stop her ready pen, and she turned now to a theme which even those who did not like her had thought beneath her. She sent "Lord Walter's Wife" to Thackeray, who was then editing the *Cornhill Magazine,* and that good man was terribly, terribly shocked. For the poem started with the Lady making most improper advances to her husband's friend. And one verse contained the word "harlot." That such a thing could come from the pure hands of Mrs. Browning!

Thackeray fell back upon an excuse which editors ever since have found a most agreeable substitute for truth. His was a "family magazine," he explained, and certainly no man could be expected to introduce "Lord Walter's Wife"

to his own family. The editor himself was broad-minded, but he must think of his public. He was quite sure Mrs. Browning would see the point. And she must not take his verdict as casting any reflection upon her distinguished literary talents.

"You see," he concluded, "our magazine is written not only for men and women, but for boys, girls, infants, sucklings almost; and one of the first wives, mothers, women in the world writes some verses which I feel certain would be objected to by many of our readers. There are things my squeamish public will not hear on Mondays, though on Sundays they listen to them without scruple. To have to say No to my betters is one of the hardest duties I have — but I am sure we must not publish your verses — and I go down on my knees before cutting my victim's head off and say: 'Madam, you know how I respect and regard you, Browning's wife and Penini's mother; and for what I am going to do, I most humbly ask your pardon.'"

"Thackeray has turned me out of the Cornhill for indecency," Ba explained gaily to her amazed friends. "But did it so prettily, and kindly, that I, who am forgiving, sent him another poem."

The other poem was "The North and the South," the last she ever wrote.

FIFTEEN

THE END OF THE IDYLL

O NE more observant of mortal ills than the healthy
Robert might have seen that the end of the Italian
idyll was approaching. For several years Ba had
been growing steadily weaker, but the progress of her disease
was so gradual that from week to week no change was no-
ticeable. Even her physicians, quite ignorant in 1860 of the
nature of tuberculosis, believed that a woman with Ba's medical history might live indefinitely. Indeed, she did not seem
to suffer as much as she had sixteen years before when there
was nothing to anticipate in life except pain and isolation
and the sterile satisfaction of work well done.

Now at fifty-four she looked younger than her sturdy,
gray-headed, white-bearded husband. Her illness kept her
slenderer than was the fashion of the day; her hair remained
black and carefully curled; her face, as she declaimed about
Italy and freedom, flushed with a vivacity that no one realized was unhealthy. She no longer walked about the galleries
nor strolled on the terrace to see the sunset, but her cheerfulness and wit remained undimmed. Any pain, any fears

of death she may have felt were well disguised under her unfailing, quiet laughter.

Of course she was sick. Even Robert could see that. He worried about it and kept his family on the move in a vain search for a spot that would restore her health as the miracle of marriage and Italy had restored it fourteen years before. But he never thought that this slow, unostentatious illness could be anything serious. When he went in search of lodgings at Siena this last year, he was much more concerned about the view from the windows than about the number of stairs that would have to be climbed to reach it. He did not remember, until Ba reminded him, that she could no longer live anywhere except on the ground floor. The apartment he had selected was at the top of impossible steps. It had to be given up, and Story found another.

The journey from Rome in June was made by vettura, and despite stops to rest and recuperate at Orvieto and Chiusi, Ba was so exhausted by the time they reached Florence that she needed a week in Casa Guidi before she could stir. Then, in July, they moved on with Landor to Siena where the Storys were waiting. Landor entertained both families greatly with his inimitable flow of reminiscence. His stories of three generations of English literary men had been well seasoned by age and appropriate lapses of memory.

But at Siena, Ba was too weak to walk across the room alone. Robert's pride in his own muscle was tempered, as he carried her from her chair to her bed, by the unpleasant realization that his burden was very light. He no longer had much time to listen to Landor's troubles, for he sat up many a night with Ba, whose cough was robbing her of sleep. So, despite the occasional periods of relief when they saw their friends as usual and talked at length of this world and more, the summer was not as pleasant as the Brownings had hoped and they were glad to return to Rome for the winter.

Rome was no better. Letters from England reported that Henrietta was very sick. Ba worried with the persistent pessimism of illness about her little sister, and for the first time her own cheerful smile was twisted a little awry. She suffered, too, with her American friends as their anxiety grew and the States drifted inexorably towards civil war. The good news of Garibaldi's triumphs was almost as bad for her as her disappointment in the cold attitude that the European powers maintained towards Italy. She was quite unable to take a calm view of anything. Whether she was praising heroism or denouncing villainy, she did it with a passionate intensity that could do her no good.

The winter passed slowly and painfully, but she concealed the suffering from Robert. It was well for him to be out in the society he so much enjoyed, she thought, and she kept assuring him that she was much better. Rest, she insisted, was all she needed. So, quite unaware that his wife was dy-

ing, Robert resumed his round of mild dissipations, the dissipation of endless talk and congenial company. He was making the most of this last season in the gay, unassuming, happy life of Italy, although he did not know that it would be the last. His reports of what went on in the world were more eagerly received in the sick room and did more good than anything else he could have brought.

Some inkling of the truth came to him when, in rapid succession, Henrietta and Cavour died. There was no restraint in Ba's mourning for her favorite sister and her favorite statesman. She brooded and agonized over the loss to herself and to Italy. Of Henrietta she could not bring herself to speak at all. Of Cavour she cried:

"A hundred Garibaldis for such a man!"

In this mood she returned to Florence. Robert was still hopeful that spring in Casa Guidi would restore to her old health the wife who had once walked with him so bravely in the mountains. But he knew in his heart that this time it was only a hope. Even Florence could do nothing for her. Her spells of coughing grew more frequent and more violent. Some were so severe that they sent Robert rushing out into the night for the doctor. Each time Ba struggled through them, but each time she was just a little weaker after it was over.

In early summer there could be no question of her being strong enough to leave Florence to escape the heat. By June she was taking ever larger doses of morphine and getting less relief from them. Her only sleep now was drugged, and towards the end of the month the effects of long illness and constant narcotic treatment were apparent. Even Robert felt that Ba must die, and he slept as little as she. Once or twice he saw her lift her hands and gaze at them dully and a little vacantly as though she were trying to puzzle out just where they came from. Once or twice as he sat beside her waiting for the morphine to soothe her, he knew her mind was wandering in the past. All his strength and health and optimism were useless. He could only sit and clench his hands and smother his own cries of pain as Ba tossed deliriously and muttered about the prison of Wimpole Street, or blamed herself anew for killing Edward, or called for Henrietta. Robert was a believer, but he did not pray much; he was too busy trying to recapture hope to pray for it.

"When I reasoned about it, there was no justifying fear," he said later, but he was not then reasonable, and he was very much afraid.

The twenty-eighth of June was one of those bright and beautiful days that recalled all their happiness. For a few hours Ba seemed marvellously to regain her health. She assured Robert that this time she was really much better, and he caught at the straw and was glad. She thought she might even enjoy a stroll on the terrace where they had walked together so often when she was strong. They were

both quite sure, as Robert carried her outside, that now she would get well. After all, she had survived so many attacks. But she was hardly on her feet, leaning on Robert's arm, than she knew she had overestimated her strength. Two steps quite exhausted her, and Robert carried her back to her sofa. Still there would be other days, they told each other, on which to walk.

"It is only the old attack," said Ba confidently, "not so severe a one as that of two years ago. There is no doubt I shall soon recover."

They had gone through a week of fear and despair and they welcomed this chance to be cheerful. Robert sent the servants and Pen off to bed, and soon carried Ba to her room. She discoursed happily about going away for the summer as soon as she should have had a few more days like this. Perhaps, she said and Robert agreed with her, they ought to give up Casa Guidi altogether. There was no denying that it was a little small for their needs and not the most convenient place in Florence. They talked of such things far into the night, and then quite suddenly Ba felt sleepy.

"I am quite comfortable if you will but come to bed," she said, but Robert would not, and he sat beside her, holding her in his arms as she dropped off to sleep.

He remained for hours, rigid and unmoving, until his muscles were stiff and his face as gray as his hair. He permitted himself the relief of movement only when Ba awoke to take her medicine, speak lightly of the trouble she was making, predict the imminence of recovery and snuggle her head more closely against his cheek.

Darkness faded, and the sun flamed into a festal glow while she slept. Robert was just thanking God for her good night's rest when the sleeper's breathing labored into noisy gasps that shook her frail body but did not wake her from her stupor. Jolted from his dreams of the future, Robert cried loudly for help and sent a maid running for the doctor. The scurry aroused Ba, and she smiled up into her husband's face. Almost as soon as she awoke, her breathing quieted.

" Shall I bathe your feet, dear? " he asked tenderly.

She smiled.

" Well, you are determined to make an exaggerated case of it! " she exclaimed, but the offer had touched her, and later Robert wrote,

" Then came what my heart will keep till I see her again and longer — the most perfect expression of her love for me within my whole knowledge of her."

The flush of her awakening still lingered in her cheeks; the pain of weeks had gone, and as she felt Robert's tired arms still around her she was quite happy, her cheek resting on his breast, her eyes gazing adoringly up at him. He thought, with a sudden twinge of sorrow, that for the first time since he had known her she looked quite girlish in the pale sunlight of early morning. In the next room Penini

slept untroubled. His parents did not give him a thought. Ba's low voice spoke only of Robert, and Robert hardly spoke at all.

"How do you feel?" he managed to ask at last.

She stirred in a movement that brought her body more closely against his; her cheek pressed a little more strongly to his bosom under his anxiously bowed head.

"Beautiful," she murmured.

She closed her eyes, and once more he forced every muscle of his body to remain rigidly still. He felt as stiff as a corpse himself, when in one horrible moment the gentle, warm pressure over his heart relaxed, the beloved head rolled slightly on his breast, and he knew that Ba had slipped from his arms.

SIXTEEN

NOSTALGIA

WHEN a confirmed optimist loses his grip on his creed, he finds more profound depths of misery than any other man can know. His sorrow deepens in proportion to the strength of the illusion that is shattered, and Robert's illusion had been strong indeed. An immense, an irretrievable loneliness settled upon him even while he still held Ba's body in his arms. He was surrounded by the most loving of friends and he had the affection of a demonstrative son, but he hardly knew that they were there. The agony of solitude, the torture of a gregarious man condemned to a dark isolation possessed him completely. He felt himself as existing only in the form of a wild and futile cry of longing for a happiness that was gone.

The Storys came rushing up from Rome to take care of the boy. They found Robert, not exactly ill and yet far from well, being nursed by the devoted Isa Blagden. On the evening Ba died, he had stumbled to her friend's house and there he remained, not quite sure of anything but his grief.

For hours on end he walked up and down, up and down in a tireless fury of useless activity, talking in a steady, despairing flow of words. He talked his friends into exhaustion as they sat, trying to soothe him, and still he talked and walked, mile on mile, without getting off the rug. He talked of his first meeting with Ba in her old room at the Wimpole Street house. He talked of the last pitiful attempt at a stroll on Casa Guidi terrace. He told them how the Austrian troops had marched down the street past them "just as she described it in 'Casa Guidi Windows.'" He talked of all the blissful fifteen years.

His unhappy friends were telling themselves for the twentieth time that they couldn't stand much more of this when he ran down at last. They managed to get him on his feet again in time for the funeral at the little English cemetery, but he was hardly interested. There was nothing of Ba left on earth that meant anything to him. He did not notice that the ceremony was quite unimpressive, most ordinary. But Story became very indignant on the husband's behalf, and wrote:

"The services were blundered through by a fat English parson in a brutally careless way, and she was consigned by him to the earth as if her clay were no better than any other clay."

Story himself did what he could to redeem the occasion from the commonplace. He left two wreaths on the new

grave, one of white roses for the woman and one of laurel
for the poetess. Then the little knot of friends closed around
Robert and took him away. He was quite docile, but again
horribly loquacious in a desperate, hopeless sort of way.

For several weeks he argued with himself about the future.
By the time he was rested and his nerves quieted a little by
Isa Blagden's careful treatment, the old optimism was returning. He could assure himself that all was now well with
Ba, and her son remained to him. He was only forty-nine;
he came of long-lived stock; the world had employment
for him.

"I shall go away," he told Story, "break up everything,
go to England, and live and work and write."

He never entered Casa Guidi again, and on the first of
August, 1861, he left Florence forever. Behind him Story
mourned their lost intimacy, Landor deplored the absence
of a sympathetic spirit and the cultured foreigners in Italy
settled down to replace the gap in their ranks by talking with
increased animation in the old vein. Casa Guidi was shut,
and though for years memories of old scenes and happiness
pulled Robert towards the place, more powerful memories
of those last weeks of anguish kept him away.

"I cannot tell how I feel about it," he wrote three years
later, "so do I change my feelings in the course of a quarter
of an hour sometimes. Particular incidents in the Florence
way of life recur as if I could not bear a repetition of them

— to find myself walking among the hills or turnings by the villas, certain doorways, old walls, points of sight, on a solitary bright summer Sunday afternoon — I think that would fairly choke me at once. On the other hand, beginning from another point of association, I have such yearnings to be there. At times I seem as if I should like, by a fascination, to try the worst at once, go straight to the old rooms at Casa Guidi, and there live and die! But I shake all this off, and say to myself (sometimes aloud) 'Don't be afraid, my good fellow, you'll die too, all in good time.' So I go on."

The journey out of Florence was filled with too many annoyances to allow time for indulging his grief. It was hot and Pen's pony, Pen's luggage and Pen himself were very difficult to transport. In seeing that both boy and pony were properly looked after and fed, Robert kept very busy. Isa Blagden, weary and in need of nursing herself, performed the last heroic service of getting him safely to Paris where Sis and his father were waiting for him. Then she took to her bed.

But Paris did not offer the peace that Robert craved. For the first and last time in his life he deliberately sought solitude. He found it at the little fishing hamlet of St. Enogat on the coast of France. The few residents of the place were much too busy scrambling for a living to bother about the stranger. He remained in the village until the autumn, recapturing the habit of thought that had made life so pleasant

in his youth when Elizabeth Barrett was only a name. He used up three or four hours of each day walking very fast over the lonely countryside. Bob artfully dissipated even more time by starting long discussions on some obscure point of long dead history. He hoped that Robert, exercising his memory in the endless wastes of their common scholarship, might be able to forget that Ba was not taking her part in the conversation. One method of filling up his time Robert did not attempt, despite his announcement that he would devote the rest of his life to Ba's son. He did not bother a bit in all these months about Pen's lessons; he did not have sufficient energy to act as teacher. The boy learned quickly enough, but he was lazy and instructing him was a chore.

The solitary hours Robert had wanted were spent in formulating more plans for the future. He finally decided that by making the next years just as different as possible from the last fifteen, he might be able to forget. He never did, but he found that the remembering was not as painful as he thought it would be. Also, the changed mode of living proved pleasanter than he had expected.

Not that he plunged into it quickly. He wanted a few months to get used to England again, the England without Ba. Coming out of the loneliness of St. Enogat, he was a little hesitant about starting at once on the course he had selected. His first glimpse of something English was of Tennyson's great beard and Tennyson himself behind it

bustling about the quay at Boulogne. Robert ordered Pen
to have a good look at the Laureate, but he himself pulled
his hat low over his eyes and, although he sat within a few
yards of his old friend, he did not speak. Tennyson bustled
off again, and Robert was able to make the rest of the
journey to London alone.

SEVENTEEN

IN SOCIETY

A NEW lion was on exhibition at the most elegant London houses in the Spring of 1862. He was an ideal society lion, so gentle a child might approach him, yet preserving all the regal dignity of his untamed, unpredictable, temperamental and unmannerly colleagues. That part of the world of fashion which deigned to patronize the arts enjoyed and was a little touched by the naive eagerness with which Mr. Browning plunged into the wearying, unexciting frivolity of dinner parties, receptions and teas.

Before he had committed himself to the task of making a new career as different as possible from the old one, his marriage and its end had begun to pass into the legends of romance. Society was pleased to see that the hero of the story looked his part. Robert Browning was fifty now, and the years had added to his good looks. His white beard was trimmed in a more orderly style than he had affected when it was black. His thick gray hair contrasted most becomingly with his large dark eyes, and because his eyes were dark men

226

and women, especially women, murmured to each other
with an awed respect that the shadow of Ba's death still
clouded them. Women who, Ba thought, had adored him
too much for decency while she was alive now set out to
remove the shadow. Robert enjoyed their efforts tremen-
dously. Grief had nothing to do with the color of his eyes.
His sorrow went much deeper than that, but he kept it in
the private places of his mind. He did not permit it to interfere with his genuine delight in feminine attentions and
sympathy.

He had not remembered how pleasant for a bachelor
existence the formality and rigid etiquette of England's
better homes could be. He had gone away a young man of
promise. He came back with the promise more than fulfilled. The city was willing to give him the reward of his
honesty — considerable praise, a loudly vocal respect and
an indifferent reading.

In youth he had rivalled Disraeli as a fop. In middle age
they both cast aside the sartorial eccentricities of the past,
and if they could be considered rivals at all now, it was in
the sobriety of their garb. Anyway, the new styles hardly
gave men a chance to indulge a taste for color. Both poet
and politician accepted the drabness of masculine clothing
and were glad to be outwardly, at least, inconspicuous.

The style suited Browning, according perfectly with the
state of his feelings, for he was quite content and very much

at peace. The sense of loneliness and bereavement which had almost smothered him in Florence just after Ba died had given way to a steady sadness which, strangely enough, was not unpleasant. He recovered old habits of thought — optimism is a weed not easily destroyed — and although an occasional cry of bitterness might escape him or a fit of mourning for the past overwhelm for a moment the solid satisfactions of his new life, they were passing phenomena in an existence devoted to proving that a great peace and a great, zestful energy were not incompatible.

The London he met in his excursions had changed enormously since the eager young Browning first attracted Macready's notice at Talfourd's party. The heavy coarseness of Georgian gayety had been borne down and overcome by the heavier decorum of Victorian respectability. Lady Howard and Lady Blessington were dead, and none had taken their places. Immorality and its even more objectionable twin, impropriety, had been banished across the Channel and only made their appearance surreptitiously in England. At least so the arbiters of British destiny fondly believed.

It was a very steady old England to which Browning returned after the kaleidoscope of Italy. Even politics were rather dull, for Palmerston held the Empire in his skillful old hands. He was in the midst of his six years of power, during which time the country hardly realized that political

parties existed. Palmerston was the Liberal leader, but the Conservatives recognized him as one of themselves by nature and inclination, and believed with the rest of England that his indomitable, cheerful, British recklessness was a fine type of statesmanship. Even Disraeli was quiet, waiting patiently for his distinguished and destined antagonist, Gladstone, to rise to full party leadership against him.

For the British public there remained only Art, the races and the growth of Empire as hobbies for a man's idle hours. A few eccentrics busied themselves with queer scientific and industrial experiments, but such topics could hardly be introduced into a polite drawing-room, and practically all drawing-rooms were polite. Most Englishmen found the races a sufficient interest, with patriotism as a convenient side line when the conversation took a lofty turn. But a considerable minority felt strange aesthetic stirrings which seem hardly credible to future generations which know them only by their photographs, their furniture and their architecture. Nevertheless, a faint urge after beauty did survive and struggle in these unlikely surroundings. It had to find an outlet somewhere, and literature, as the most fashionable of the arts, was the favored choice of the aspirants to culture.

Browning stepped easily into a comfortable place among the writing men who were setting marks for the future to shoot at largely because it came quite naturally to them to observe all the reticences that convention dictated. They never — or hardly ever — questioned the essential soundness of these conventions. Browning particularly was very happy within their limits and a little uncomfortable outside of them. So he and the others never felt called upon to preach their views. It was no fun preaching when all the world agreed.

He had expected to devote the lonely hours of his life to educating Pen. But there were fewer and fewer lonely hours, and besides he was an impatient pedagogue. He was glad to turn the boy over to tutors, for he had no gift in stirring a lazy child's interest in study. He took such an interest for granted, and when he discovered his error he gave up the task, saying philosophically:

" I am relieved about Pen, by knowing the very worst of the poor boy, to wit that he won't work, or perhaps can't."

As invitations thickened the morning mail and his literary peers clustered around to elaborate their ponderous beliefs, Browning was glad to relinquish a too active rôle as teacher to just one child. Pen's drawing lessons still found him regularly in attendance, but that was because the teacher was Anne Egerton Smith, one of the women adorers, who talked music with the father while she kept an eye on the pupil's pencil. The poet had always loved music.

He liked travel even better, and although he avoided Italy for a few years, the rest of the Continent saw him frequently

230

as he followed the excellent custom of fleeing from London
to recuperate from one season's decorous festivities in time
to take on the next. He went abroad because he had so many
invitations to English country houses that he could not accept them all. It pleased him greatly to be able to make this
explanation, beaming at large while he recounted the quite
surprising sum of his personal popularity. Cold rains that
kept younger men by their own firesides could not daunt
him. Three nights running on which his son refused to
brave the elements found Robert walking out to dine with
Lady William Russell, the Sartorises and Lady Palmerston.

He managed to keep his afternoons and evenings thus
comfortably filled with happy distractions which he was
able to believe were solemn duties. The true Victorian always knew that he owed certain such pleasures to his Position in Society. But the mornings remained, and at fifty
Browning was discovering a use for the time between
breakfast and lunch. Work could be done in the mornings.

Never before had he permitted himself regular hours of
labor, although Ba had often told him that he owed that
much to his Position in Literature. He had been sceptical
about his Position in Literature, but no modesty could be
proof against the obvious evidences that it was improving.
He had written nothing in the last few years to account for
his increasing prestige. His wife's death had led romanticists
to pick up the books by the man she had loved, but Brown-

ing's sentimental appeal was never strong enough to keep such readers. He gave them headaches where they looked for heartaches.

The true explanation of his improved Position lay in the uninterrupted play which London afforded his gregarious nature. He had taken his place in the first of literary societies, and was no longer just a name and a reputation for incomprehensibility. Authors, critics and the patrons of both saw him so often that they could not forget his existence, so they spoke about him, wrote about him, even read some of his poetry. He came in quite naturally for that pleasant give and take in the reviews which writing men find so valuable and at which the envious outside the friendly circle snarl with the bitterness of men whom there are none to praise.

Enough of this variety of admiration was lavished upon Browning so that the proprietors of the *Cornhill Magazine,* seeking for a successor to Thackeray, offered the editorship he had resigned to the poet. He was very much surprised and not quite sure whether or not he should feel flattered for the offer was accompanied by the explanation that the owners thought Mr. Browning could attract writers to the magazine.

"I who could never muster *English* readers enough to pay for salt and bread!" he exclaimed.

He could not make up his mind for a long time. He was

delightfully conscious of being able to decline with dignity or accept with profit. Nothing so material as a salary had been mentioned, but he had assurances that the remuneration would be adequate. He was quite determined that he would not except less than Thackeray had received. That part of it was very tempting to a man who was saying he had " a son who may want no end of money."

True, Browning knew nothing of the technique of editing, but no one has ever refused an editorial job because of conscious ignorance. Every man, especially every writing man, is quite sure that he can do such work with his left hand. Browning was no exception. Indeed, he thought, it would be very pleasant to show the world for once how articles should be selected. He also had a very great curiosity about the mechanics of the medium which he had always scorned for his own works.

" It requires merely editing," he wrote to Story, explaining that if he accepted he would not have to print any of his own poems and thus outrage his old principles.

The " mere editing " would, he was sure, leave him plenty of time for the serious effort that seemed to be demanded by the gratifyingly increased popularity of his earlier books. In the end, however, he decided against sacrificing even a small part of his freedom. He declined the Cornhill offer with thanks, and the last chance he ever had to earn a substantial part of his living went to join the madder dreams of his courtship in the land of might-have-been.

More gratifying than offers of editorships with salaries was the recognition bestowed upon him by established authority on learned matters. All his life Browning possessed that exaggerated respect for Universities, their opportunities and their honors which no University man ever acquires. He and the world of letters had once felt that the inscription, "by Robert Browning, author of Paracelsus," on the title page of a book lent that book distinction. But Robert now gained a dignity of which he was far more proud than of having written "Paracelsus." He received an honorary degree and the subsequent edition of his collected works was given to the public as "by Robert Browning, M.A., Honorary Fellow of Baliol College."

He followed this edition up the next year with a volume of new poems, and there was a mild flutter of appreciation for "Dramatis Personae." Browning remained quite modest under it, for he had always known that he was one of "God's elect," and that it was just a matter of time before others found it out, too. They had known it for many years in Italy, and Robert was loyal to his memories.

"I see plenty of new wonderful people," he said in acknowledging his new popularity, "but none as interesting to me as the old, even though not particularly wonderful."

As a mark of his fondness for these old friends, he devoted

many of his mornings of work to reading and correcting Story's book, "Roba di Roma." Robert not only found the publisher and prepared the manuscript for the printer, but he read the proofs and spoke of the book's excellence at dinner-tables to the famous men he was meeting everywhere.

For he went everywhere. He was present while the upright Gladstone charmed select and pure audiences with his disarming smile, his magnificent voice and his correct sentiments. He heard Matthew Arnold telling of the pleasures of the simple life while he sipped his wine and gazed complacently about a well appointed room. He shared Dickens's extravagance on festal occasions, and was easily as boisterous as the novelist when they pushed through celebrating crowds and watched holiday illuminations. After one particularly large evening when all England was rejoicing over the marriage of the Prince of Wales, Robert noted the fact that the van from which they had failed to see the fireworks had cost five pounds. He also noted the fact that Dickens paid. His love of music prompted him to seek the society of such performers as Joachim and Halle, and they were sufficiently impressed by his knowledge of their art that he was able to boast:

"I make them play at parties where I meet them."

From such gayeties Browning was sometimes turned by a realization of his responsibilities. He had two, Pen and

Wilson, and he could not always decide which was the more onerous. After all his years of working to establish a position in the learned world — he was sufficiently paternal that he could on occasion delude himself that all he had done was for the sake of making his son's life easier, not for any fun he got out of it himself — Pen had failed in his entrance examinations at Baliol. It was a bitter disappointment. The boy was amazed and remorseful when he saw how hard Robert took a little thing like failure. He studied very diligently for a time and won his way back to his father's good graces by getting admitted to Christchurch.

Wilson presented a different problem. After her mistress's death she brought Fernando back to England and opened a lodging-house. Lodgers did not materialize, and the savings of a lifetime were quickly dissipated. Fernando added to her troubles. She had lost for him her chief charm, sixteen pounds a year, and he declined to exert himself so long as he had a wife capable of earning a living. Wilson had English ideas about a husband's duty to support his wife, and the couple quarreled bitterly in the empty house which was so unattractive to prospective paying guests.

Meanwhile their former employer was making a home for himself in London. He took a house in Warwick Crescent, a quietly superior neighborhood, and sent to Florence for the furniture from Casa Guidi. He indulged in an orgy of reminiscence as he arranged the old belongings in their

new places. Each chair and table, each picture, each bit of tapestry had its dear associations. He remembered where each had been obtained, how Ba had exclaimed over it, how cheap it had been. The new home lacked just one thing, the old servants. Robert offered to take Wilson and Fernando back into his employ, but when he saw them he was glad that they refused. Wilson's troubles, he thought, had made her a little mad, and he could not approve of the callousness with which Fernando treated her. They wanted to go back to Florence and have a business of their own. Robert sent them off, but the business was a failure. Fernando in his native city could take good care of himself, but he refused to support his wife. George Barrett offered to take the responsibility, but Robert protested:

" I cannot allow him to take my business on himself."

The poet finally settled an allowance of ten pounds a year on Wilson for the rest of her life.

With Pen safe in Christchurch and Wilson provided for, he could devote himself without interruption to the pleasures of Society. He took such a boyish delight in them that he would never have suspected he was growing older had it not been that death gave him an occasional reminder. His father died, quietly as he had lived, supplying his son to the very end with bits of historical lore that all the rest of the world had forgotten. The old man had been very happy for years, free of the hated bank, able to read all day and

talk all night. He was tended by a devoted daughter and could brag as much as he liked about his talented son.

His sudden, short illness took them by surprise, for although he was eighty-four, he had never seemed old. Robert hurried over to Paris, where Bob had lived since his retirement from business, just in time to gladden the old man's last hours by sitting at the bedside. Bob's last thoughts were that the children should not tire themselves by sitting up with him, and he died smiling at them affectionately.

"He was worthy of being Ba's father — out of the whole world only he, so far as my experience goes," Robert would say, and all who heard him knew that the son properly appreciated the father's perpetual sympathy and cheerfulness.

Later the famous library came over to London, and Robert wondered what he could do with so many books. Sarianna came too, transferring her devotion to her brother, and tried to make a home for him as she had done for their father.

Two years later Arabel Barrett, with whom Robert had in the months following Ba's death entered into bonds of friendship which consisted of eulogizing the perfect wife and sister, died in his arms as Ba had done. He mourned her as a lost link with his past; now there was one person less who had known to what heights women could rise.

EIGHTEEN

ON PARNASSUS

ROBERT'S mourning for Arabel and his father was intensified by regret that they had not survived to witness the triumph which he soon achieved. He had been driving himself steadily at his poetry, and the Roman murder story grew and grew. He learned with amusement that Trollope, poor old Tony, had not been able to see a story in the case. Mrs. Baker had found some old records of the trial and sent them to the novelist, who had returned them with polite, unenthusiastic thanks. Browning could afford to be a little scornful of novelists. He himself knew good story material when he saw it better than they did, although he had more difficulty telling it in a form which men would read.

But the longer he worked on this one, the more he saw the magnificence of its possibilities. He took his time. Years rolled on, thousands upon thousands of lines dripped off his pen and huge piles of manuscript accumulated as the author told his story again and again and again.

" The Ring and the Book " was published in four volumes,

one a month for December and November, 1868, and January and February, 1869. By the time the last one was off the press, Browning was famous. For sheer volume alone — and mass was a highly valued literary quality in those days — it surpassed anything of its generation. But more than that, it had the distinction, shared with few enough poetic masterpieces, of being a story told well, beautifully. It was read, it was talked about and it gave impetus to the pleasant literary pastime of discovering the man Browning in every character he portrayed.

It was a literary shibboleth just then that no man could write sincerely, convincingly, of any character without partaking to a considerable degree of that character's nature. Yet how, the poor puzzled devotees of this creed demanded, could Browning partake of so many and such diverse natures? Granted their premises, the obvious deduction was that he possessed a mind of such devious and tortuous complexity that normal men could not hope to understand. The truth, of course, was that Browning was an unpretentious, completely natural person, so unassuming that he did not know learning such as his was unique, so free of any perplexing dogmas of his own that he could reflect with photographic accuracy the most varied characters and yet absorb nothing of them. His own complete simplicity made it possible for him to portray more subtle natures. With all his masterly gift for words and for interpreting the work-

ings of any human mind, he remained quite set in his own sober ways, cautious of innovation and so satisfied with his own make-up that he never bothered about introspection.

Meanwhile publishers had been hearing of the magnitude of the work Mr. Browning was doing. They were so impressed that a year before "The Ring and the Book" was finished, its author was gloating:

"Booksellers are making me pretty offers for it. One sent to propose, last week, to publish it at his risk giving me *all* the profits and pay me the whole in advance — 'for the incidental advantages of my name' — the R. B. who for six months once did not sell one copy of his poems. I ask £200 for the sheets to America and shall get it."

As the four volumes came out, they were snapped up with the eagerness usually reserved for the latest extra on a murder trial. Of course that is just what it was, but so artfully embowered in blank verse that the public obtained the cultural delight of literature along with the emotional thrill of a murder and the "fight for life." Indeed, the subject smacked so much of journalism that Carlyle remarked admiringly, and a trifle patronizingly:

"What a wonderful fellow you are, Browning! You have written a whole series of books about what could be summed up in a newspaper paragraph."

The publishers had been a little doubtful of the monetary success of such a stupendous mass of reading matter, and

the first edition was rather small. Its popularity was sufficient that the author, answering Isa Blagden's complaint that he did not send her a copy, was obliged to apologize and explain that he did not have one to send.

"You see," he said, not without some pride, "I was never in the position before of one who had ' sold all the books.' "

Despite this success, a note of the old criticism crept into the reviews. Browning was becoming increasingly sensitive to the taunt of obscurity, and he lost his temper when accused of carelessness or a deliberate attempt to confuse. He had actually been so circumspect he had the Astronomer Royal confirm the fact that a new moon really did shine the night in 1697 when Giuseppe Caponssachi and Pompilia Franceschini fled from Arezzo to Rome. He objected volubly to the charge of obscurity when the complaint was based on an ignorance of words which were so common they were in Johnson's Dictionary. People who aspired to read poetry, he believed, ought to have memorized Johnson.

Maria Bathoe was helping prepare a new dictionary, and thought the poet would be pleased to have extracts from " The Ring and the Book " included.

" I find a considerable number of words whose meaning is by no means clear to me," she wrote him. " As it is important for the purpose in view to fix the precise signification, perhaps you would fill up the enclosed column with the exact meaning."

The column contained thirty-eight words, all in Johnson, such as "fleshliness," "imposthume," "effraction," "votarist" and "inexpugnable." Browning was annoyed, exclaiming:

"If Elizabeth Garrett, M.D., wrote to a physician to say that the words "aneurism, comatose, hemorrhage, abscess" and many others wanted explanation and that she was working for the complete Dictionary of Medical Science, would you not tell her something more impolite than what I am about to tell Mrs. Bathoe, that people who intend to supplement Johnson would better read him first of all."

What he actually told the lady, and quite kindly, was that she would find all the puzzling words in Johnson or in "yesterday's *Times* and *Athenaeum.*"

He jested, a little bitterly, about his reputation, but he could not change his ways, and in rare moments of doubt he wondered if he really was obscure. Soon after "The Ring and the Book" was published, the Chinese Minister gave the sober householders of Warwick Crescent a glimpse of oriental splendor as, clad in his native robes of state and attended by a retinue such as Browning's neighbors had never before seen, he came to honor the poet with a visit. His Excellency spoke no English — a degree from an occidental university was not yet a prerequisite to diplomatic preferment at Peking. Robert welcomed the gorgeous entourage with some embarrassment; he was still unaccus-

tomed to honors like this. But the diplomat quickly put him at his ease by explaining through the interpreter that he came to call merely as one poet to another.

" What is the nature of Your Excellency's poetry? " Robert asked with keen interest.

" Chiefly poetic enigmas."

" Ah," said the Englishman ruefully, " I salute you as a brother."

Nevertheless, when he counted up his blessings, criticism was more than offset by the growing admiration which Browning was exciting among young men. He was very proud of it and took every opportunity, even after Pen had left the University, of going down to the rooms he had taken for himself as a Fellow of Baliol. He loved to move about among the awed students and speak to them paternally about poetry and scholarship.

The booksellers of Oxford and Cambridge reported gratifying sales of Browning's works. Youths gathered eagerly around the poet at balls and dinners. The rising generation wrote him long and gushing letters. He found their homage charming, for he had reached that most delightful of all ages, the age of reminiscence. Here was a new audience for him, and he made the most of it.

The young, however, only supplemented the audience without which he could not have been happy, a select group of intelligently sympathetic women to whom he could talk

as he could to no man, not even to Dommett when " Waring" came back from New Zealand after thirty years to
resume the old friendship as easily as though it had never
been interrupted. To Isa Blagden, Anne Smith, Lady Marion
Alford, the aged Lady William Russell, Browning freely
poured forth the thoughts that were kept hidden from the
men he knew — his fears and hopes for his son, the rare
doubts that all was for the best in this best of all possible
worlds, his occasional fits of boredom, his stories of days
so happy that the unsubstantial memories were strong
enough to remove all flavor from the present triumphs. The
listeners soothed him, flattered him, lectured him prettily and
sent him back to the world with his faith in life restored and
reënforced so that in arguments over whether good or
evil predominated in this world, he was able to apologize
for his determined stand for good by saying in humble
tones:

"Well, I can only speak of it as I have found it myself."

Men could not bolster up that faith, even the wisest of
them. Browning was one with his contemporaries in setting
women upon a higher plane of goodness and purity than
was attainable by the stronger sex, battling, as they believed,
amid so many more temptations than ever beset a lady. Besides, he had recognized the normal need of men to turn to
women as their confidantes, and he was glad that it was so.
Years ago he had written:

" God be thanked, the meanest of his creatures
　Boasts two soul-sides, one to face the world with,
　One to show a woman when he loves her! "

The side he showed the world was that of the man of
letters and of substance, too, who held up his end in a
political discussion, even when his admired friend Gladstone
was present. Browning, indeed, enjoyed a reputation for a
rather wide political vision. He had lived so much on the
Continent that he took a European rather than the prevailing insular view of affairs.

His sympathy for France as he watched the " wretched
impostor," Napoleon, bring the Second Empire crashing
down in ruins upon a brave people was so great that he
actually overcome his scruples against magazines. He sold
" Hervé Riel," a martial lyric of French heroism, to the
Cornhill for £100, which he quite rightly considered an immense price, and sent the check to swell a fund which was
being raised for the benefit of starving Paris.

He had had a glimpse of what the conditions were, for
the Franco-Prussian war had caught him and his French
friend, Joseph Milsand, at St. Aubin. The Englishman's dismay as the Prussian armies shattered the proudest regiments
of France was almost as great as Milsand's, but Browning
took some comfort from the final union of Italy when the
French troops marched out of Rome, where they had for

years kept the Pope secure in the Quirinal, and Victor Emmanuel marched in.

Milsand hurried up to Paris to remove the valuables from his house, which stood outside the fortifications and must fall easy prey to the rapacity of the advancing Prussians. He returned to St. Aubin to urge his friend to leave France while he still could. Already it was almost too late. The news of Sedan was spreading, refugees clogged the roads and it was with difficulty that Browning reached Honfleur. The only accommodations he could find for the voyage across the Channel were on a cattle boat, and he was glad to get even such primitive quarters. He was reminded of his earlier trips to Italy.

In the same year he published two very different books. " Prince Hohenstiel-Schwangau, Saviour of Society," may be taken for just what its author intended it to be, a very fair explanation of Louis Napoleon's motives and excuses, and one of the author's rare excursions into contemporary affairs in search of material. He was convinced that he was wise to stick to the past when he began hearing criticisms of his work. The Emperor's friends denounced the poem as a dastardly attack on betrayed greatness. His enemies cried out in anger against Mr. Browning's shameless defense of so much iniquity. The poet himself remarked with satisfaction:

" I am told my little thing is succeeding; sold 1,400 copies in the first five days and before any notice appeared."

The other poem was much more scholarly, recalling to the public that Mr. Browning was " learned in the Greek." This was " Balaustion's Adventure," an interpretation and a translation of Euripides' " Alkestis." The idea was suggested to him in the course of a dinner by the Countess Cowper. It appealed greatly to the poet, for Ba had once translated Euripides, too. The public again was appreciative, and Browning wrote:

" Twenty-five hundred in five months is a good sale for the likes of me."

He understated the case. Twenty-five hundred in five months was an unprecedented sale for him. " Balaustion's Adventure " was the most swiftly appreciated of any book he ever wrote, not even excluding " The Ring and the Book," and Carlyle exclaimed:

" Ye won't mind me, though it's the last advice I may gie ye, but ye ought to translate the whole of the Greek tragedians — that's your vocation."

The sage of Chelsea was right. It was the last advice he gave his young friend, and Browning did not take it. He passed his sixtieth birthday with no pause in the activity of his life. Every day he turned out his twenty or thirty lines of poetry, the normal daily allowance, and continued to cement his abundant friendships. Whenever a party flagged, it was a recognized practice to challenge Browning's oft-repeated boast that he could find a rhyme for any word in the

THE SALON AT CASA GUIDI

English language and put it into a verse. He usually guaranteed to do it in less time than his listeners used to select the word. In this way he evolved prodigious quantities of doggerel, and he was a little proud of some of it. He took the pains to preserve the lines written in response to a challenge to put "Timbuctoo" into verse:

> "Ah, massa, such a fiery oss
> As him I rode at Timbuctoo!
> He would not suit a quiet boss!
> Him kick, him rear, and him buck too!"

Dining with the Laureate, he once repeated his usual offer, and Tennyson, who knew something of the difficulty of rhyming, gave his colleague, after much thought, "rhinoceros." With less thought, the guest chanted:

> "O, if you should see a rhinoceros
> And a tree be in sight,
> Climb quick, for his might
> Is a match for the gods — he can toss Eros!"

Such frivolous activities pleased Browning immensely, and his booming laugh and loud voice provoked one fellow guest to inquire as to the identity of "that too exuberant financier person." And Disraeli dismissed Gladstone's friend, of whose works he was quite ignorant, with a contemptuous

snort about " second rate fashionables." He saw Robert here
and there about the town and expressed this opinion of him
and the conversation in which he delighted:

" Browning, a noisy, conceited poet; all the talk about
pictures and art and Raffaelle and what Sterne calls the Cor-
reggiosity of Correggio."

The poet repaid the scorn, believing with most Liberals
that the Prime Minister was the greatest rogue and hypocrite
in politics. " Triply cased in brass," he said of Disraeli, and
accused him of having

" No use

In men but to make sport for you, induce
The puppets now to dance, now stand stockstill,
Now knock their heads together, at your will
For will's sake only."

The gibe of " second rate fashionable " was not one Robert
could take lightly, even from the man who had been invited
to take a chair in the Queen's presence. Moreover, it was un-
deserved. Although Browning found more intellectual pleasure in talking of " the Correggiosities of Correggio " with
Carlyle, Ruskin, Tennyson, Rossetti, Matthew Arnold, Leighton, Millais and the other leading artists of his time, the
most aristocratic houses in London also valued his society,
and he gratified his pride by being truly a " first rate
fashionable."

His place in the world was recognized by offers of the
Lord Rectorship of the Universities of Glasgow and Saint
Andrews. He declined, both because of the expense involved
in such honorary places and because the only public speaking he enjoyed was the convivial, if formal, language of the
after dinner speakers. One of the affairs he enjoyed most in
all of a quarter of a century of assiduous dining out was a
banquet at Oxford. He was so impressed that he noted down
some of the toasts given and commended the addresses made
on each subject. The glasses were filled, and emptied, to
Baliol, the University, the visitors present, Parliament, the
clergy, the bar, literature and science ("dear Mat Arnold
replying"), and the Fellows and Scholars. Robert could not
remember ever having attended such a feast of reason and
flow of soul.

He was also greatly pleased about his domestic fortunes.
It appeared that Pen's laziness and charm were merely ex-
pressions of an artistic temperament. Just what form this
aesthetic leaning would take had been doubtful. The boy
had written some verses of which Robert thought but little,
and he followed them up with an ambitious effort of some
six hundred lines chronicling an adventure of his vacation
in France.

"Nor would I give much for this," the not very proud
father wrote to Isa Blagden. "This is an ultimate product,
but considering the boy's all but absolute ignorance of poetry,

it was very welcome proof indeed of what may still be in him."

That Pen should be so ignorant of his father's art was not surprising. With the sound common sense which distinguished him among poets quite as much as his literary ability, Robert had sedulously refrained from encouraging his son to attempt the writing of verse. He understood quite clearly what a handicap would be imposed upon a youth expected always to live up to the traditions of such a parentage as Pen's. Consequently Robert was jubilant when the boy developed both skill and interest in painting. All the rest of his life he was prolific of advice about subjects for his son's canvases and the way in which they should be treated.

He was, however, much too busy to devote to Pen the time and pains his own father had expended on his education. His American following, always greater than that in England, was beginning to pay real dividends. Ever since "The Ring and the Book," his name had such drawing power across the ocean that it was worth a publisher's while to get the brief advantage of an "authorized edition," even if it should be pirated within a few weeks. The publication of "Hervé Riel" had broken down much of Browning's opposition to magazines. He still refused most offers from such sources, but the *Pall Mall Gazette, Poet Lore,* the *Century,* the *London World* and the *Athenaeum* were favored with some pieces of which he did not think highly. He was

quite pleased, too, to sell American rights to the *New York Times* for "The Inn Album," a poem of some three thousand lines, and the paper published it serially, seven columns at a time.

He had found an ideal vacation ground, the little village of Collonges near Geneva, where he spent four summers with Sarianna and Anne Smith. Tourists almost never bothered to invade the picturesque cluster of little houses at the foot of Mount Saleve, but there was an excellent inn, the countryside was delightful and Geneva was readily accessible when the urge for crowds and shops became irresistible.

But the fourth summer was the last the poet enjoyed in the Swiss retreat. On a particularly divine evening in 1877 he and Miss Smith walked on the terrace planning a big adventure for the morrow. They would climb Saleve's rugged face and from the summit attain what local mountaineers pronounced an incomparable view of Mont Blanc and Lake Geneva. They retired early, for they were to start at dawn, but when dawn came Anne Smith was dead. She had died quite painlessly in a sudden heart attack while waiting for her friend to join her, and Robert had lost the best beloved of his confidantes.

Sadly he fled from the vulgar, bewildering tumult that surrounded the dead woman and set out alone on the climb two were to have made. He deadened his sorrow by the

arduous exertion of toiling upwards along almost perpendicular slopes, and at the summit he found that peace which men must feel as they gaze from a height over the majesty of mountain ranges spread out before them. As he looked, the inspiration for a poem came to him, but the emotion that prompted " La Saisiaz " was not new. He had experienced it and expressed it much more simply when, just after Ba died, he wrote on the flyleaf of her Bible Dante's words of Beatrice:

" Thus I believe, thus I affirm, thus I am certain it is, that from this life I shall pass to another better, there, where that lady lives of whom my soul was enamoured."

He went back to London, to the ceaseless round of fashion and wit, and found ample solace in his fame and friends for the loss of the woman who had most completely in these last years shared his thoughts and listened to his beliefs. But when the season ended, he did not go back to Collonges.

Seventeen years had passed since he had fled from Casa Guidi, and now he yielded to the longing to see Italy once more. He was quite happy renewing old friendships, observing the changes that the years had wrought, revisiting old shrines. But there was one shrine he avoided. He could not bring himself to go to Florence.

NINETEEN

THE HARVEST

THE fame Browning won in the seventies was harvested for rich rewards in the eighties, that securely happy decade which seemed destined to last forever. The older he grew, the more he enjoyed life. Years could not dull the keen delight he took in being asked out to dinner and in being honored for his works. More and more his opinion, whether he argued about Home Rule for Ireland or the pre-Raphaelite school of poetry, was greeted with polite attention; even critics became deferential if not laudatory. Their respect, which once would have elevated a younger Browning to the pinnacles of pride, did not conciliate him now. In his garden he kept two geese, " Edinburgh " and " Quarterly " after those two powerful journals of contemporary opinion, and he was very fond of calling these pets by name.

He was getting arrogant, almost as opinionated as he had been in his brash 'teens. At seventy he could not adjust himself to the idea of being a great man, just as at eighteen he failed to realize that he was not a great man. He was not prepared for the part any more. He resented contradictions; they offended his dignity so much that he once forgot himself and threatened during a dinner to throw a decanter at Forster's head. The critic had ventured to cast some doubts upon the veracity of a woman Robert quoted. The poet believed such doubts amounted to questioning his own veracity, and he was quite prepared to fight.

Despite these rare outbreaks, he did not lose his charm of manner. His pride did not carry with it contempt of others, and already such a great punctilio as he had learned when Victoria was a girl had become a little old-fashioned. In a dignified, handsome, white-haired old man the amenities of which he was so prodigal were much admired, especially as they provided a pleasant contrast for his works. These were not old-fashioned. Younger readers were finding Browning's dramatic monologues much more intoxicating than the daintier froth of less thoughtful poets.

Their admiration, exuberantly expressed, delighted him when shortly after his seventieth birthday he came down to Oxford to be presented with a D.C.L. Cheers, enthusiastically unbecoming to the solemnity of the occasion, greeted his appearance. One youthful admirer of his " Red Cotton Nightcap Country " dropped from a balcony a real red cotton nightcap which landed jauntily askew upon the poet's white head. The masters of Oxford were outraged.

Such an indignity committed upon so distinguished a visitor would be punished appropriately, they promised. But Robert had been pleased. The incident showed that someone had read " Red Cotton Nightcap Country " and he could forgive a reader even greater indignity than this.

He interceded zealously for the culprit, and his successful argument was a characteristically Browningesque bit of history. He " reminded " the learned Dons of something they had never known, that centuries ago such pleasantries were an official part of university honors, carefully perpetrated lest the recipient acquire too great a sense of his own importance in the scheme of things.

Two years later Edinburgh followed Oxford's example, and Browning travelled to Scotland to be invested in another scarlet robe. At the attendant festivities he was so pushed about by autograph seekers and by the merely curious that his hostess, accustomed to the modest shrinkings of less durable celebrities, asked anxiously:

" Do you object to all this adulation ? "

" Object to it! " the frankly insatiable seeker after happiness exclaimed in great surprise. " No, I have waited forty years for it, and now — I like it."

His ostentatiously robust health accounted for this ability to enjoy a life that other men, no less vain, found exhausting. He could stand for hours, shaking hands with all comers and conversing with them volubly about anything. When it was over, he felt no weariness, rather a pleasant exhilaration at having been the center of attraction. He attended every big dinner of the season, and many that were not so big. No theatrical opening, no concert, no private view of an artist's latest works could pass without Browning's helpful presence. He became the greatest first-nighter as well as the greatest diner-out of his age.

Browning Societies were springing up all over England and America, a unique tribute for a poet to receive in his lifetime, and these earnest students of his work added heavily to his correspondence. But his regular, daily composition of twenty or thirty lines, his tireless social activities, his exertions on behalf of Pen's paintings and his voluminous letter-writing were not enough for his energy. He took up seriously the study of Spanish and Hebrew. At an age when most men pride themselves on not having forgotten much of what they learned in youth, Browning was eagerly acquiring new knowledge with which to embellish his last poems.

The physical strength which had been the boast of his youth was still so little impaired that on his trips to Italy he thought nothing of walking for five hours without a halt and at a brisk pace over the rough mountain paths. Sis shared these arduous rambles — she had the family constitution — but their younger friends found the Brownings much too strenuous. After a day of mountain climbing that

258

sent men of half his years to their beds, Robert would sit up half the night talking.

At seventy-four he was still such a steady wanderer about Europe that the Royal Academy offered him the post of foreign correspondent. He accepted that honor as he did all others, with eager gratitude, and flung himself into the task of keeping England informed about the progress of Continental art and letters with an energy that prevented the office from seeming purely honorary.

Warwick Crescent had for many years been regarded by its most distinguished resident as merely a temporary home. In 1887, Browning decided that he was old enough to make a permanent retreat for himself and Sarianna. He took a house in De Vere Gardens, a spacious and comfortable mansion, and here for the first time he found room to display all of his father's six thousand books. Here, too, he could bestow to good advantage the furniture, the paintings and the innumerable knickknacks he had picked up in many decades of travel. His domestic instincts were gratified by the thousands of little details that made up the burden of moving. He was genuinely happy buying little things for the house, superintending the placing of books and pictures. In his study he had most of the furniture from Casa Guidi's salon, so that he could work among the reminders of his happiest years.

But as soon as De Vere Gardens was in just the order he

wanted, he dashed off to Italy. He was not yet old enough
to settle down. Besides, Pen was to marry an American girl,
Fannie Coddington of New York, and had already made
up his mind to live in Venice. Robert applauded his choice
of a home and of a wife. Two years before he had nearly
bought a palace in Venice for his son, but the owner had
backed out after the bargain was sealed. Robert sued to force
fulfillment of the contract, but discovered that the old walls
were badly cracked behind their gorgeous tapestries and
hastily withdrew his action at law. Now he was glad of it,
for the new Mrs. Browning was possessed of money. The
children bought the magnificent Palazzo Rezzonico, one of
the finest in all Italy and once the home of that Cardinal
Rezzonico who in 1758 became Pope Clement XIII. The
huge white marble pile towered up from the waters of the
Grand Canal. Carvings and little balconies on all three
floors adorned the pillared front. It was more than usually
comfortable inside with its immense high rooms and broad
staircases, and the poet found it a very pleasant place to
stay. That his son should have picked a foreign daughter-
in-law for him was not displeasing either. He had always
liked Americans and disapproved of English girls. He did
not like the looks of the young women at home.

"I think very few English women pretty," he complained.
"Their complexions I don't care for and their Elizabethan
aquiline noses and chubby cheeks I dislike. I only saw one

beautiful girl, that I should so designate, at two great houses last season (I mean I saw her twice) but had not the curiosity to ask her name."

He left his son in Italy to return to London for a season which was in that year enlivened by highly voluble evenings at De Vere Gardens. No dinner table in the city could boast a more elevating flow of conversation than Browning's. At the head, the host, his silver hair gleaming in the candlelight, his gray eyes still sparkling with the vivacity of youth, carried the company along on a steady stream of give and take which many guests found so absorbing they did not notice the very excellent food that the poet set before them.

Browning was getting old, but he had only one worry. He feared biographers as he had once feared critics, and he went to a good deal of pains to collect letters he had written to old friends. He destroyed as many as he could get his hands on, retaining only the sacred correspondence with Ba. These he knew should belong to the world, for he had given them to Pen with the comment:

" Do as you please with them when I am gone."

He refused to supply even close friends with biographical material when they wished to capitalize his fame with a " Life and Letters." Such books, he said, were shameless invasions of privacy. No man should be thus exposed until he was decently dead, and not even then. He rebuffed acquaintances gently, all except Edmund Gosse to whom he confided some corrections of a few of the more glaring inaccuracies that were occasionally used by the reviewers. But when strangers suggested anything of the kind, he allowed his passion full rein. To a man who had obtained several of Ba's letters and proposed to print them, Robert wrote with such unrestrained rage that his friends were alarmed and the intending biographer so amazed by the barrage of abuse and threats that he was glad to let the matter drop without further correspondence. Browning fumed for weeks, explaining:

" Think of this beast working away, not deeming my feelings, or those of her family, worthy of notice. It shall not be done if I can stop the scamp's knavery along with his breath."

And still later:

" What I suffer with the paws of these blackguards in my bowels you can fancy."

It was not that he feared anything scandalous could be raked up from his past life. But he wanted to be known only through his works. There, he would insist, was to be found all that was immortal of him, and if more were asked it would be presented in his new book. He allowed the rumor to spread that this work was to be autobiographical, and indeed he really thought it was. " Parleyings With Certain People of Importance in Their Day " was awaited eagerly. It came out in 1887 and was a distinct disappointment to

those who looked for frankness. The *Times* began its review with the warning:

" The supposition that Mr. Browning's new work was to be of an autobiographical character is entirely erroneous."

Only some of the Browning Societies and a few university scholars who have followed them have attempted to dispute this verdict. Into the book they have read a variety of meanings, largely because they would not take the plain interpretation where an involved one is possible. The " Parleyings " are autobiographical only in that they purport to elaborate certain of the author's views in the course of telling a story or depicting another character. He had done the same thing many times before, and he had done it better, for in his best monologues action and color dominate thought.

In the " Parleyings " Browning believed he was explaining his own mental development to some extent, but it is obvious that a man so little given to introspection could never analyze such a complex process as that development had been. If any one man's influence can easily be followed through the years of Browning's rise to the literary heights, it is that of his father. But the poet never knew it. He thought Landor and Shelley, of whose characteristics only the barest traces are discernible in his poems, had done much to make him what he was. But even these two were not mentioned in the " Parleyings."

Undoubtedly his wide reading of obscure authors had been

largely responsible for the scholarship which was his out-
standing quality, and the new book was merely a recognition
of it. But much more than reading had gone into the making of the Browning mind. His friends, his love, his health,
his calm and happy life, his unusual, zestful, lusty joy in just
being alive and that indefinable something which the world
hails as genius were surely of as much importance as Bob's
library. If the " Parleyings " are to be taken as autobiographical, they give a very poor picture of the man who wrote
them, of a man who has never been surpassed in giving
very good pictures of other people. For the " Parleyings "
portray only the bookish, learned side of Robert Browning.
It was not surprising that fashionable London, the London
that knew the man best, the London that prized him as one
of themselves but did not care for his poetry, failed to recognize the portrait.

The new book, although not a great success, did not check
the demand, especially in America, for Browning's poetry.
Wondering a little at his own prosperity, he refused an offer
of £400 for a short poem, or what for him was short. On
another occasion he returned a blank check from a London
publisher. To this generous gentleman, reiterating his opposition to periodical literature and explaining that he rarely
overcame it, he said:

" My wife liked it. She liked to be with the others, but I
have steadfastly refused."

It was on his wife's behalf that he gave way to the last great anger of his life. Edward Fitzgerald, the translator of "Omar," had for many years kept a diary which, now that he was dead, his friends considered worthy of publication. The editor, although eliminating some passages, neglected to suppress the paragraph in which nearly thirty years before Fitzgerald had noted:

"Mrs. Browning's death is rather a relief to me, I must say; no more Aurora Leighs, Thank God! A woman of real genius, I know; but what is the upshot of it all! She and her sex had better mind the kitchen and the children and perhaps the poor."

Browning read, and in a less temperate liver the reaction might well have produced a stroke of apoplexy. In Ba's husband it produced a raging fury that found vent in a savagery not usually associated with his poetry. That Fitzgerald was long dead himself, that he had been one of the kindest, gentlest, most lovable and least obtrusive of men, that he was the sort of scholarly, conversational gentleman in whose society the poet most delighted, that his friends still remembered him with the deepest affection — all this meant nothing to the maddened Robert. He rushed some lines off to the *Athenaeum,* for once he wanted just the sort of rapid publicity a magazine could give, and on July 13, 1889, the subscribers to that highly respectable periodical were shocked to read under the signature of the respectable Robert Browning:

" I chanced upon a new book yesterday;
  I opened it; and where my finger lay
  'Twixt page and uncut page, these words I read, —
  Some six or seven, at most, and learned thereby
  That you, Fitzgerald, whom by ear and eye
  She never knew, thanked God my wife was dead.
  Ay, dead, and were yourself alive, good Fitz.
  How to return you thanks would tax my wits.
  Kicking you seems the common lot of curs,
  While more appropriate greeting lends you grace;
  Surely to spit there glorifies your face, —
  Spitting from lips once sanctified by hers."

TWENTY

"A DEATH IN THE DESERT"

A S Wilkes was no Wilkite, I am quite other than a Browningite," Robert once protested to Edmund Yates when some of the philosophies of the Browning Societies were attributed to "the Master."

It was as harsh a remark as he ever made about the organization which both flattered him and subjected him, especially when it was young, to a good deal of chaffing. He could not resent seriously anything such devoted admirers might do, so long as they did not trifle with his private life, and they had far too much respect for him to do that. But dimly he saw whither the Browning Societies were tending, and the vision frightened him a little. For he was a literary man, not a philosopher; he wanted to be read, not just studied. Therefore, the hasty and emphatic repudiation of the charge that he, too, was a Browningite. The denial was as prompt as if he had known that the Societies, after destroying his popularity, would perish themselves from the very lack of that popularity, which was their entire subsistence and real reason for being.

The seed of the Societies was in those Browning evenings and Browning readings in America of which Ba had been so proud when her husband's works first attained fame across the Atlantic. Originating in the sort of spontaneous admiration which is the aim of all writers, the impromptu " evenings " developed form and substance and, worst of all, ritual. It was this last that made them dangerous. The first offshoot of the " evenings " was a Browning club established by Hiram Corson, professor of English literature, at Cornell University. Harried by generations of students to whom anything labelled a classic was a bore rather than a pleasure, he conceived the really excellent pedagogic expedient of stimulating interest in his subject outside the classroom. He was so successful, thanks to Browning's strong appeal to the youth of that day, that when he visited England he explained his idea with a certain pardonable triumph to some of the poet's friends.

The idea germinated in the fertile minds of Dr. F. J. Furnivall and Emily Hickey, ardent admirers of Browning from early days and possessed of the means and leisure necessary for the task of making Browningites out of Browning fans. They communicated their plans to their hero and he innocently approved — the moment of apprehensive insight was not vouchsafed him until later. So in July, 1881, a neatly printed prospectus was mailed to a select list. Neither the poet nor his friends saw anything incongruous in this method of promoting literature along the lines favored by salesmen of mining stock. Browning, it is true, refused to have anything to do with the matter except to admit un-officially that he was not displeased, while Dr. Furnivall and Miss Hickey were rather proud of their high-minded mo-tives, set out in the prospectus thus:

" This Society is founded to gather together some, at least, of the many admirers of Robert Browning, for the study and discussion of his works, and the publication of papers on them, and extracts of work illustrating them. The Society will also encourage the formation of Browning Reading Clubs, the acting of Browning's dramas by amateur com-panies, the writing of a Browning Primer, the compilation of a Browning Concordance or Lexicon, and generally the extension of the study and influence of the poet."

Even before this prospectus came from the printer, the idea had aroused some amusement in irreverent circles. The general notion was that the Society would be a group of pale but earnest satellites revolving in awed respect around the blazing glory of the poet's orbit. Therefore, this para-graph was added to the little folder:

" To remove misunderstandings that have arisen, the Com-mittee state that anyone joining the Society is not in any way pledged to indiscriminate admiration of Browning, but is only supposed to hold that the poet is profound enough in thought, noble enough in character and feeling, eloquent

and interesting enough in expression to deserve more thorough study, and a far wider circle of readers than he has yet had. The Committee wish for frankness of expression in all papers, etc.; and they give notice from the first that every writer in the Society's publications is to be held as speaking for himself or herself alone, without any responsibility whatever on the Committee's part."

Besides a recognition of Browning's genius, there was one other qualification for admission. It was neatly stated along with plans for meetings and in a pompous profusion of capitals as follows:

" The Society will consist of all Subscribers of 21 shillings a year. It will meet once a month from October to June (except in December) on the 4th Friday of every such month at 8 P.M. at University College, Gower Street, W.C., for the Hearing and Discussion of a Paper or Address on some of Browning's poems or his characteristics. The Society's best Papers and Reports of its Discussions will be printed either in full or in a *Monthly Abstract* sent to all members as funds allow."

For the extension of their idea to all parts of the country, the founders offered this inducement to the Provincial Browningites:

" The Committee are anxious to appoint as *Local Honorary Secretaries* those students of Browning in or out of London who will undertake either to get up Browning Read-

ing Clubs in their respective Districts, — after the example of Professor Corson, who has directed one in his University (Cornell) for the last five years, — or otherwise promote the study of Browning in their neighborhood as opportunity offers."

With great dignity, the founders undertook to reprove those superficial scoffers who had dared to criticize their idol.

"Without entering on the vext question of who is the greatest living poet," they wrote, leaving no doubt at all as to how they would answer the question if sufficiently urged, "Mr. Browning's admirers are content to accept the general verdict that he is both one of the greatest and *the* most thoughtful. . . . If on some great themes Browning's thoughts have not been more easily apprehended, may this not come from want of faithful study, default of deadened minds? At any rate, the Browning student will seek the shortcoming in himself rather than in his master. He will wish by conference with other students, by recourse to older scholars, to learn more of the meaning of the poet's utterances; and then, having learnt, ' gladly wol he teche,' and bring others under the same influence that has benefited himself. To this end *The Browning Society* has been founded."

The response which this document received was amazing. When the first meeting was called to order by Dr. Furnivall at University College on October twenty-eighth, there was a

large and solemn audience looking at him. Browning was not in the house, but he had sent a message of good cheer. There was a reverent hush over the assembly, the hush of men about to launch upon this troubled earth a new soap or a new religion. Indeed, it was a little difficult to decide whether they regarded their project in a business or a pious light, but they put into it the fervor of both. Whatever else they may have felt, they certainly had nothing of the pleasure lovers of books feel in settling down with a piece by their favorite author. That was the last thing the Browning-ites wanted. However, in their own staid way they had a most enjoyable evening, and there was a well-bred patter of applause for the first of the Browning Society Papers, " On the Characteristics of Browning's Philosophy and Poetry," by the Rev. J. Kirkman, M.A.

Of course, it was rather ridiculous, but Browning's sense of the absurd had never been very keen. He never had so much sense of humor as to be able to see the fun of a situation in which he figured as a hero, and besides he could not help thinking of the critics who had been so vitriolic years ago.

" What a world of width between such people and Mr. Kirkman! " he exclaimed to Dr. Furnivall after perusing the clerical gentleman's Paper.

So the Browning Society under Furnivall's careful guidance prospered and was imitated. It thrived so abundantly

that Robert within a year was able to write gleefully to the
President:

"I am beginning to enjoy the results of the institution of
the 'Society' in the evident annoyance it is causing my dear
old critics who have gone on gibing and gibbering at me
time out of mind."

But there was another, and in many ways a deeper pleasure that the Society afforded. For years he had been embarrassed by questions as to just what he meant in such and
such a line of such and such a poem. Earnest, determined
readers, most of them women, would put a damper on the
best of parties by backing him off into a corner and demanding full, complete and erudite interpretations before
they would let him get away. He had never known just how
to avoid such encounters or how to act during them. Now
the problem was solved. Puzzled admirers no longer had
any terrors for him. When pressed to set at rest the doubts
that had arisen, he would chuckle cheerfully, wave a hand
airily and reply gaily:

"Ask the Browning Society. They can tell; I can't."

Meanwhile the Society had spread to America in name as
well as form, and in the lush atmosphere of the States attained its finest flower. Every town with any literary pre-
tensions at all boasted its Browning Society. A wave of culture was sweeping through the land in the eighties and
nineties, and a multitude of estimable ladies who had once

found cooking and sewing and husbands and babies all-absorbing topics of conversation now exchanged painfully elevated ideas on the poetry of Mr. Browning. His syntax was discussed with as much eager animation as in these un-regenerate days is devoted at Book of the Month Clubs to the rather more personal foibles of Frank Harris.

From New England to Texas, women, and men too, gathered at regular intervals for the worship of whatever particular brand of philosophy they chose to find in Browning's poetry. Here he was an apostle of the great humanities; there he was the prophet of progress; in another place he was exalted as one who preached the purest Christianity.

The disciples agreed on only one thing, that Robert Browning was a great philosopher. They were quite wrong, for they confused scholarship with philosophy. Browning was a poet — the fact seems almost to have escaped the Browning Societies completely — and he used the philosophies of other men as a matter of course without even subscribing to them himself, much less originating them. If he ever had a strictly new thought of a kind to qualify him as a philosopher, he kept it to himself, and he was not a man to practice that sort of intellectual reticence. It is safe to say that every time he was called a philosopher he was libelled. As a scholar he probably had no equal in England after his father died, and of this there is plenty of evidence in his books. But such distinction was not enough for the Society members. They in-

sisted that " the Master's " poetry must contain all things for all men, even qualities that would prevent its being poetry.

For seven years Browning spent a good deal of time writing to Furnivall letters in which he attempted to explain simply what the Browning Society wanted explained elaborately. He had but little success. The Papers of the Browning Society continued to be involved and labored efforts which had all the faults of obscurity which could ever be attributed to the man whose meaning they sought to clarify but none of the beauty with which he could endow even an obscure thought. They are dull reading, but fortunately for the student of literary phenomena, the titles sum up admirably the content of the work.

Among those considered worthy of perpetuation in the published discussions of the Browning Society is one, a rather average production, entitled " A Grammatical Analysis of 'O Lyric Love.' " It is not a parody. So lost to all sense of poetry had Browning's followers become that this Paper was considered a real contribution to the better understanding of the Browningesque " philosophy." Not a single member seems to have realized that if there is one sure way to destroy both a lyric and a love it is by grammatical analysis. Nothing was too comprehensive, too vague or too complex for the analysts to attempt. Consider such discursive articles as " Browning's Views of Life," " Browning's Estimate of Life," " The Idea of Personality as Embodied in Robert Browning's Poetry." On the other hand no subject was too insignificant, no reference too trivial for the most extensive research and voluminous arguments. Long Papers, displaying evidence of hard study, were read on " The Line Numbering, etc., in ' The Ring and The Book ' " and " The Moorish Front to the Duomo of Florence in ' Luria,' pp. 122–132." Of this last Paper when it was proudly displayed to him in type, Browning cried:

" I never heard nor dreamed there had been any such notion at any time of a Moorish front for the Duomo — it was altogether a fancy of my own."

Even the Papers which practiced vivisection on Browning's tenderest passages or sought to reduce to an anaemic philosophy his most vigorous lines were not the worst. It was deemed necessary to compile a " Browning Phrase Book." The work was undertaken by the Boston Society, most ambitious of the American organizations and a fair specimen of the tribe, above the average if anything, for Boston was not trying quite so desperately for culture as some of the western cities. Bostonians thought they had it. The Society was founded in the winter of 1885–86 with Henry Stone as President. The next year the Boston group was so well-established that it was able to have a Higginson, Col. Thomas Wentworth Higginson, as Mr. Stone's successor. Under the sway of a man who had the family ability for organizing such things as banks and religions, the Society

stepped out briskly on the career which made it a success for quite a few years.

The parent Society in London languished and died in 1893, but in Boston the work of interpreting the poet was still going strong long after the turn of the century. The other American Societies were by no means defunct either, and their papers poured off the provincial presses just as fast as in Boston. But the Bostonians had the Phrase Book.

Just what purpose this work was designed to further is not quite clear. Probably it was an end in itself. At any rate it represented a stupendous amount of tabulation, for it is an alphabetical list of nearly every word Browning used, with a quotation from his works illustrating his use of it. The compilers, for example, have taken the month of May and quoted Mr. Browning's illuminating line on that subject, " This May — what magic weather." That seemed to make it all quite clear to the Boston scholar. The book, it is plain, was not designed to give a key to the peculiar uses to which Browning sometimes put a word, nor to elucidate his employment of unusual words. " Could " is listed, and after it the lines:

> " No genius but you could have been, no sage,
>   No sufferer — which is grandest — for the truth."

And " should " is there with the example:

> " What he should have been,
>   Could be, and was not."

Strangely enough " would " is not in the list, although in his sixteen volumes Browning used it more than once. An oversight, no doubt. Anyone who has flipped the pages of this very solid book and obtained a glimpse of the staggering number of words it contains will be churlish indeed not to pardon the slip and make obeisance to the industry of the editors.

Many critics considered it unwise and a little ridiculous to start such an institution as the Browning Societies while the poet was still alive. But in fact the Societies owed their lives to his vitality and they did not long survive him. The little cliques, each pretending to comprise all those who could understand the poetry of Robert Browning, honored him in his lifetime. But after his death they performed the greatest disservice that any writer can suffer. They effectually repelled the young, to whom the living man had made such a strong appeal, and with every paper they published, the alienation of public affections was carried a bit further. By fostering the legend that Browning wrote philosophy, not poetry, his too serious adherents insured for him the apprehensive, deliberate neglect of casual readers and turned all that was best of his long life out to die in the arid wastes of public indifference. His was a tragedy, although he did not live to see it, well captioned by the title of his own poem, " A Death in the Desert."

In America the Browning rage continued as long as the

craze for culture. But when women began to take up golf and politics and business, they had no more time and less inclination to linger in the desert. The social life of dozens of communities shifted from the Browning Society to the country club, and soon only a few students were left to penetrate into the unknown in pursuit of the elusive Browning meaning. And like all desert rats, they were rather silent people, speaking a language of their own when they did speak. They could never describe to others the really splendid relics they had found buried in the sands of oblivion, and the literate world, if it thought of Browning at all, thought with the parodist:

> " Ah, did you once find Browning plain,
> And did he seem quite clear,
> And did you read the book again?
> How strange it seems and queer! "

TWENTY ONE

THE ABBEY

AS Browning rounded his seventy-seventh birthday, he offered thanks to the God in whom he sincerely believed that his pursuit of happiness had been successful. He had everything he could hope for in this world, and he had lost none of his power to enjoy it. He was still what Landor had described him forty years ago in those lines:

> " Since Chaucer was alive and hale,
> No man has walked along our roads with step
> So active, so enquiring eye or tongue
> So varied in discourse."

In 1889 there was only one sign of weakness, and by that time Browning's reputation was so unquestionable that no one saw it. His poems, the " Lines to Edward Fitzgerald " excepted, were losing the vigor of youth. He could no longer rise to the heights attained in the dramatic monologues of his prime. But this was hidden from himself as well as from his public. The old will, the old energy, the

old optimism were, if anything, stronger than ever. He had never been so busy. He revised and published a complete edition of his works in sixteen volumes. He was working on a new book of poems. And in the intervals he seriously considered writing " Sordello" all over again to make its meaning quite clear. Only some doubts as to just what that meaning had been fifty years ago kept him from attempting it. He only talked of it, and in the end decided to leave ill enough alone.

In Society he was such an imposing figure that royalty, in the person of the Shah of Persia, was impressed. Lord Rose-berry, following the British custom of attempting politely to overawe an Eastern potentate who may become dangerous, had invited all England's greatest men to meet the Persian, and had urged them to wear all the decorations to which they were entitled.

Browning in the scarlet cloak of an Oxford D.C.L. stood out so conspicuously among the Peers, a little awkward in their unaccustomed robes of state, that the Shah asked to be presented, and spent most of the evening talking poetry instead of oriental politics. He even asked for a copy of Mr. Browning's poems, and Robert, who had nothing suitably bound for such a personage, was obliged to make a special trip to town next day to secure one.

At the end of this pleasant season, he put the manuscript of the new book, " Asolando," into the hands of Smith and

Elder and departed happily for Italy. A part of his yearly pilgrimage of late was to Asolo, whose beauties he flattered himself he had discovered on his first visit more than half a century before. He still spoke of it as his favorite resort. He was so enthusiastic about the charm of the little town and the surrounding country that Mrs. Arthur Bronson, an American confidante who had replaced Anne Smith and Isa Blagden, both dead now, in the poet's affections, took a villa in Asolo and entertained him there on his last visit.

But Browning decided he must in future have a home of his own in Asolo. It would be pleasant, he said, to feel that he was again permanently domiciled in the land of his happiest years. So he applied to the municipality for permission to buy part of the old castle grounds. He desired, he explained, to make for himself a retreat for his declining years. He had apparently forgotten the purpose of De Vere Gardens. The municipality was flattered, but the law was the law. Foreigners might not without special dispensations own such national treasures as Robert proposed to acquire. There could be no doubt a dispensation would be granted to him, the distinguished writer, the early friend of Italian liberty, the singer of Italian aspirations. But there was much red tape to be unwound. Browning was satisfied. There was no hurry. He felt that he had many years before him.

"I shall soon depart for Venice on my way homeward," he wrote in October.

He was always glad to be in Venice. Pen was charmingly deferential. There were enough old English and American friends to permit of plenty of dining out. And he had never lost his fondness for the canals. Long walks on the Lido, long rides in gondolas, long talks over the dinner-table — these made up the happy sum of his days.

On an afternoon in late November he walked a little too far and a little too fast. He rested by taking a gondola back, and the chill damp wind bit to his bones. The next day the doctor pronounced it bronchitis, and by evening the world was being informed that the great poet was very ill.

Lover of life though he was, he did not make a fuss about dying. He was a good patient, chatting as usual and insisting that he was quite comfortable. He acknowledged that he could almost feel the strength running out of his old body, but there was no pain, and he could look back on nearly seventy-eight wonderful years. In all of them he would change nothing — well, almost nothing.

Within two weeks he was being kept alive only by the unusual vigor that had been his pride ever since he could remember. But that was being rapidly exhausted, and in the morning of December twelfth he suffered several fainting spells. Early in the afternoon a messenger arrived from

Asolo with the news that the municipality had just voted him permission to buy the land he wanted. The old man smiled weakly, but he knew it was too late.

A little later came a more important message. December twelfth was the day of "Asolando's" publication, and George Murray Smith telegraphed:

"Reviews in all this day's papers most favorable. Edition nearly exhausted."

They read the telegram to the dying man, and for a moment he seemed to revive. After all the early years of neglect, the reviews were favorable! After all the middle years of recognition without book sales, the edition was nearly exhausted! He sighed happily and murmured:

"How gratifying."

They were the last words Robert Browning ever spoke. Thinking how gratifying it all was, he passed quite easily into a stupor from which his physicians could not arouse him. For a little time his big chest rose and fell unevenly as he gasped for a few last breaths. Then that much exertion became too much for his strength. He was still unconscious when he died.

All the honors in which he had rejoiced in the last years of his life were eclipsed by those paid him at his death. Venice allowed the body to depart only after elaborate ceremonies, and on the walls of the Rezzonico Palace, the city placed a tablet with the inscription:

A

Roberto Browning

morto in questo palazzo

il 12 Dicembre 1889

Venezia

pose

"Open my heart and you will see
Graved inside of it, 'Italy.'"

On the last day of the year his body was placed in the
Poet's Corner of Westminster Abbey. The offer of a national
funeral had come just after Pen learned that the cemetery
in which his mother was buried had long been closed. He
accepted gratefully, but declined the further offer to have
Ba brought back to the Abbey too.

That British public — "ye who like me not (God love
you!) " — liked Robert Browning now. The court, the Government, the nobility and literature were all strongly represented as the solemn Church of England service was read
over the grave of the dissenter. Nothing could have gratified
the man Browning quite so much as the presence of that distinguished array. Nothing could have gratified the lover
Browning more than to hear the choir singing Ba's own
verses, "He Giveth His Beloved Sleep." But what would
have more deeply touched the poet Browning was the reverent crowd of common people, chiefly very young men and

285

women. More than most, it was a crowd come to honor a writer rather than a mob curious to see a show. It was the crowning tribute to his genius.

Already the quality of that genius was obscured by the zeal of commentators. While he was still alive, men could retort to the interpreters, " But what does Browning say himself? " and usually Browning said nothing. But when the man was dead, the poet's friends had their way with his works. No one could pick up a volume of his poems without realizing that careful reading was required. But it remained for his admirers to spread abroad the legend that careful reading was not enough, that intricate and painful analysis was necessary too.

Within a very few years, while Tennyson was still universally acclaimed, Browning was remembered only as a perennial dinner guest, as the hero of an unique love story and as a poet who wrote verses to be studied, not enjoyed. Sarianna, who died at the age of eighty-nine, lived to see the day when her famous brother's anecdotes were no longer repeated in society, or at least no longer credited to him, when his too exuberant laugh and childish joy in parties were quite forgotten. Ten years later when Pen, too, was dead, the love story of his parents was a little dim in public memory. Today even the reputation for obscurity is rather vague. There remains but one more step to complete the circle. Some day a bright young man is going to " discover " Robert Browning.

Archer, William — *William Charles Macready,* 1890.

Berdoe, Edward — *The Browning Cyclopaedia,* 1916.
The Boston Browning Society Papers, 1897.
Browning, Elizabeth Barrett — *Complete Works,* 6 vol., 1900.
Browning, Elizabeth Barrett — *Letters,* 2 vol., 1898.
Browning, Elizabeth Barrett — *Letters to Richard Hengist Horne,* 2 vol., 1877.
Browning, Elizabeth Barrett — *Letters of Robert Browning and E. B. Browning,* 2 vol., 1899.
Browning, Robert — *Complete Works,* Florentine Edition, 12 vol., 1910.
Browning, Robert — *Correspondence of Robert Browning and Alfred Dommett,* 1906.
Browning, Robert — *Letters to Miss Isa Blagden,* 1923.
Browning, Robert — *Letters to Various Correspondents,* 2 vol., 1895.
Browning, Robert — *Some Lamb and Browning Letters to Leigh Hunt,* 1924.
The Browning Society's Papers (London), 3 vol., 1881–91.

Catalogue of Pictures, Drawings and Engravings; Autograph Letters and Manuscripts; Books and Works of Art, the Property of R. W. Barrett Browning, Esq. (Deceased), 1913.
Carlyle, Jane Welsh — *Letters,* 2 vol., 1883.

Carlyle, Thomas — *Letters to John Stuart Mill, John Sterling and Robert Browning,* 1923.

Cary, E. L. — *Browning, Poet and Man, a Survey,* 1899.

Chesterton, G. K. — *Robert Browning,* 1903.

DeVane, William Clyde, Jr. — *Browning's Parleyings,* 1927.

Dickens, Charles — *Letters,* 2 vol., 1879.

Douglas, James — *Robert Browning,* 1903.

Forster, John — *Life of Charles Dickens,* 1873.

Forster, John — *Walter Savage Landor,* 1869.

Froude, James Anthony — *Thomas Carlyle,* 2 vol., 1884.

Gosse, Edmund W. — *Robert Browning, Personalia,* 1890.

Gould, George M. — *Biographic Clinics,* 1903.

Griffin, W. Hall — *The Life of Robert Browning,* 1910.

Hawthorne, Nathaniel — *Letters to William D. Ticknor,* 2 vol., 1910.

Hawthorne, Nathaniel — *French and Italian Notebooks,* 2 vol., 1871.

Hawthorne, Mrs. Sophia Amelia — *Notes in England and Italy,* 1869.

James, Henry — *William Wetmore Story and His Friends,* 2 vol., 1903.

Kemble, Fanny — *Further Records,* 1891.

Kemble, Fanny — *Records of Later Life,* 1884.

Key, Ellen — *Människor,* 1913.

Landor, Walter Savage — *Letters,* 1899.

Letters of the Wordsworth Family, 3 vol., 1907.

Lubbock, Percy — *Elizabeth Barrett Browning in Her Letters,* 1906.

Macready, William C. — *Diaries, 1833–1851*, 2 vol., 1912.

Madden, R. R. — *The Literary Life and Correspondence of the Countess of Blessington*, 2 vol., 1855.

Martineau, Harriet — *Autobiography*, 2 vol., 1877.

Molineux, M. A. — *Phrase Book From the Poetic and Dramatic Works of Robert Browning*, 1896.

Orr, Mrs. Sutherland — *The Life and Letters of Robert Browning*, 1891.

Ossoli, Margaret Fuller, Marchesa d' — *Memoirs*, 2 vol., 1852.

Phillips, M. E. — *Reminiscences of William Wetmore Story*, 1897.

Rannie, David Watson — *Wordsworth and His Circle*, 1907.

Richards, E. F. — *Mazzini's Letters to an English Family*, 1920.

Ritchie, Anne Thackeray — *Records of Tennyson, Ruskin and Browning*, 1892.

Rossetti, W. M. — *Some Reminiscences*, 2 vol., 1906.

Sharp, William — *The Life of Robert Browning*, 1890.

Tennyson, Hallam, Second Baron — *Tennyson and His Friends*, 1911.

Waugh, A. — *Robert Browning*, 1900.

Whiting, Lilian — *The Florence of Landor*, 1905.

Whiting, Lilian — *The Brownings, Their Life and Art*, 1911.

Wordsworth, Dorothy — *Journals*, 1904.

Wordsworth, William — *Memoirs*, 1851.